Praise

"D.R.E.A.M. *is relatable… It is inspiring, funny, thought provoking, and challenging. I truly love the saying:* Dreams Do Come True For People Just Like YOU!"
    -Tranere N.

"*No matter what your age, Jeremy has given us a blueprint to a better and blessed life. These pages can be your personal pep rally to dream!*"
    -Julena E.

"*Jeremy Taylor paints a very real picture of opportunity in his book,* D.R.E.A.M. *Page by page, anecdotal evidence abounds, proving that success can be reality if you just dare to dream!*"
    -Kyla B.

"D.R.E.A.M. *is incredible! Each chapter not only shares a key principle of success for any area of life, but it can inspire you to take action immediately towards your goals!*"
    -Luke C.

"*It is one of my all-time favorite books! Jeremy Taylor has poetically written a nonfiction book that will captivate the imagination of those who read it! I believe this book will bless countless lives all around the world!*"
    -Tasha E.

"This book is incredible - great storytelling, which allows me to relate to the struggles and successes of entrepreneurship, at a young age. Jeremy Taylor gives good life lessons through personal experiences. The acronym D.R.E.A.M. is genius!"

    -Jason A.

"This book proves that it takes childlike faith to D.R.E.A.M. It's been a healthy reminder that in life anything is possible!"

    -Jaala M.

"I started reading this book and I couldn't stop! I'm impressed and inspired to pick up and finish some of the ideas God has put in motion in my life that I haven't yet completed!"

    -Kevin B.

"So many people today live in fear of pursuing their dream because they can't imagine how they will get there. Jeremy's focus is on building belief in your vision and dream first and letting the how come later. This is the true secret to great success."

    -Martha C.

"D.R.E.A.M. is an incredible and rousing book that you won't soon forget. Each chapter is as authentic and genuine as the author himself. Regardless of your vision or goals in life, Jeremy Taylor's words will inspire you to pursue them with passion and conviction."

    -Kurtis P.

"An inspiring read that encourages us to get excited and take action with childlike faith knowing that success is attainable for all who dare to D.R.E.A.M."
          -Chris E.

"D.R.E.A.M. can change your life. It reminds you that you are the master of your future. Jeremy Taylor did an amazing job writing this book, making it both fun to read and inspiring."
          -Selina W.

D.R.E.A.M.

Dreams *Do Come True* . . .
For People *Just Like YOU!*

Jeremy A. Taylor

Foreword by Clifton Lambreth

D.R.E.A.M.

Dreams *Do Come True...*
For People *Just Like YOU!*

First Edition

Publisher: Jeremy A. Taylor

ISBN-13: 978-1505852479
ISBN-10: 1505852471

Scripture quotations are from:

The Story ESV Bible. (2013). Wheaton: Crossway.

Wilkinson, B. (2000). *The Prayer of Jabez: Breaking Through to the Blessed Life* (p. 92). Colorado Springs: Multnomah Books.

Table of Contents

Dedication

*Most people who decide to grow personally
find their first mentors in the pages of a good book.*
-John C. Maxwell

This book is dedicated to The DREAM Network, and to the many people, like you, who dare to dream big dreams. It is my wish and my prayer that this book will help take you from where you are to where you want to be so, you can live the life you've always imagined. You have a gift; go share it with the world!

Acknowledgements

To my Father in Heaven - You chose to not leave me in the mess. You came for me, you picked me up, and you placed me here. The death of your Son, Jesus Christ, saved me, and your Holy Spirit sustains me. Your plan is perfect and it is good. Thank you for writing this book and allowing me to put my name on it.

To my parents, Teresa Mitchell and Dwight Taylor - Thank you for accepting the responsibility of raising me. The prayers that you prayed and the sacrifices you made molded me into the man I am today.

To my siblings, Dewayne, Jessica, Michael, Cyera, and Tiana - You make being a brother one of the best jobs on the planet.

To the Taylor Gang - You gave me my first lessons on how to get knocked down and get back up. I credit my toughness to your tough love.

To my grandmother, Phyllis Calhoun - You've always been one phone call away.

To Jason, Mark, Brandon, Tasha, Luke, Jon, and Amanda - It takes courage to be a winner. Thank you for sharing your stories and allowing me to highlight what makes you special to me.

To Kurtis Parson - You epitomize the word friend.

To Michael Edwards and D.C. Clement - You believed in this book and my ability to inspire and encourage people before I did.

To Clifton Lambreth - Thank you for shepherding me through this entire process. I am a better person because of you.

To Chris Estes - You taught me not only how to *get* my hopes up, but how to *keep* my hopes up.

To Greg Bibb - Everyone needs someone to look up to, literally and figuratively. For me, I'm glad you allowed that person to be you.

To Billy Gregory and Ron Derr - You are God's representative in your respective career fields and communities. Your examples of faith and leadership have influenced me greatly.

To Randall Shofner, Paul McQueary, Troy Young, and Keith Adkins - Thank you for placing the basketball in my hands at each level of my playing career and giving me an opportunity to grow and lead.

To Susan Blevins - Your homework every single day taught me how to put first things first at the kitchen table as soon as I got home.

To Michael Jordan - You were one of my childhood heroes. You taught me how to compete.

To Les Brown - You showed me what it looked like and sounded like to have passion behind my purpose.

To Mark Batterson - You taught me how to submit my plans to The Lord and pray God-sized dreams.

To Gaylon Yarberry and Cindy Beals - You saw something in me and gave me a chance to teach and coach. Taylor County High School and Warren East High School will always be in my heart.

To all of My Students and Athletes - I prayed for you before I ever met you. I learned more from you than you learned from me. I am grateful for each and every one of you.

To Ken Brailsford and Rod Larsen - Your vision and opportunity has provided a platform for me to become the very best version of me.

To my faith family: Living Hope Baptist Church - Thank you for bringing me in and teaching me how to live hopeful and be helpful.

To the editors - Thank you for the hours you traded to make this book something worth reading.

Our truest life is when we are in our dreams awake.
-Henry David Thoreau

Foreword

Jeremy Taylor's *D.R.E.A.M.* is packed with inspirational stories and great informational truths that have been time tested.

This acronym reminds readers that *choosing to dare, taking risks, staying excited, remaining committed to action* and *allowing momentum to work for you*, can help accelerate your journey toward the realization of your dreams.

Jeremy's transparency of the stories he shares should provide hope to all who read. His creative approach to sharing his story and others stories is an effective way to share great truths, that if applied, will aid in your success on your way to significance. The inspiration of this book is delivered through numerous stories of individuals faced with ordinary challenges and obstacles that we all find ourselves struggling with daily. Several stories involve seemingly impossible consequences, but by observing the strategies used (and applying them to your journey) provide readers with hope, that if they can do it, we should try also. This book also reminds us that while there is hard work to becoming successful, we should all remember to have fun and seek joy in our lives.

The following pages provide a strategy for balancing your efforts toward success and significance. It is an easy read for most people, but as Jeremy reminds us, some things are *easy to do*, but also just as *easy not to do!* Investing the time to read *D.R.E.A.M.* is a choice you will have to make; I hope you choose wisely. If you choose to read it and apply it, I can assure you that you are on your way to realizing your dreams faster and you will travel further. I promise you won't be disappointed. I hope you get to meet Jeremy along your journey. He will be the blessing for you that he has been for me and many others.

The final question is: *"What are YOUR dreams and are you willing to pursue them passionately?"*

Remember the *D.R.E.A.M.* acronym along your journey:

D - Dare ✓
R - Risk ✓
E - Excitement ✓
A - Action ✓
M - Momentum ✓

[handwritten: FRES S WE ARE ON OUR WAY! LET'S GO!]

I hope you choose to read this wonderful book and share it with your friends and family!

-Clifton Lambreth

*Clifton Lambreth worked over twenty-six years for the **Ford Motor Company** in various capacities. He was a rainmaker at every position he held. Throughout his career with Ford, he consistently was a **top performer receiving prestigious awards** and distinctions including **five Ford Drive for Leaders awards and three Diversity Leadership awards**. Clifton was one of only three people at Ford worldwide to receive the **2008 Ford's Leadership Award**. As **a highly sought after public speaker**, Clifton tours the nation and has **spoken to thousands of individuals in over 150 business and community groups** on success principles and "Doing the Right Thing." Clifton has authored and published three **top-selling books:** *Ford and the American Dream, The Return to Greatness* and *The Ad Man.*

Do You Have a *D.R.E.A.M.*?

The future belongs to those who
believe in the beauty of their dreams.
-Eleanor Roosevelt

Have you ever had something you wanted to do - something that really moved your heart? I'd be willing to bet that you have. It kept you up late at night. It woke you up before your alarm clock sounded off. It may have been something you couldn't explain. There was a fire burning in your belly. You were ready to go for it, and then... you talked yourself out of it. You decided you weren't qualified, you figured you didn't have enough money, or you thought you didn't know the right people. You may have even looked around at other "successful" people and began comparing yourself to them. You even rationalized why it was okay to not go for it. Or maybe you're like a young lady that shared with me in conversation one day, "I had dreams, but I thought those were things that you could never achieve." Do something for me, please. Take a deep breath and smile. I have some good news for you pertaining to your dream!

Before I share the good news, do one other thing for me. This will help me help you. Open your mind. It's been said that the mind works best like a parachute, when it's open. I want you to have a mind that's open to everything and attached to nothing. You may not agree with everything I have to say and you may not even like some things I say. That's okay; I'm not asking you to. Here's what's important:

the simple truths in the pages that follow have taught someone like me, a small guy from a small town, how to dream and dream big. After fumbling around in my 20s, I not only discovered the ingredients to a recipe for pursuing my calling with a clear focus and unmatched level of excitement, but also what it means to attain success - a life of significance. To give you a little heads up, it requires failure.

SUCCESS REQUIRES FAILURE

So, back to that dream of yours we were discussing. Here's the good news: you are one **DECISION** away from manifesting it. The decision to do it. In my opinion, most people who have ever achieved a great success, began with little to nothing. You don't have to have it all figured out, and you don't have to know all of the details. It's not required that you see the entire staircase before taking the first step. The first step all big dreamers and super achievers have taken was the decision to go for whatever was brewing in their heart.

If you decide to do what you can with what you have, you will soon find out that whatever else you need along the way will show up in due time. Henry David Thoreau told us, "If one advances confidently in the direction of his dreams, and endeavors to live the life which he has imagined, he will meet with a success unexpected in common hours." Don't allow the "How is it going to work?" or "How is it going to happen?" questions to paralyze you. The *how* is none of your business at the moment. It will reveal itself when the time is right.

Every great dream begins with a dreamer. Always remember, you have within you the strength, the patience, and the passion to reach for the stars to change the world.
-Harriet Tubman

Once upon a time, I knew where I wanted to go (or at least I thought I did), but I didn't know how I was going to get there. It wasn't until I experienced a few things and met a few good people that I figured out what it meant to D.R.E.A.M. My story may not knock your socks off, because it's not the grandest of grand "rags to riches" story. However, in this book, I'll share with you a simple, practical acronym that I picked up along the way, despite my personal imperfections and less than perfect conditions, and a few stories that I hope will help you on your journey.

As you move through the pages, I encourage you to spend time reflecting between chapters on who you are, what your desires are, and what your life values are. This collaboration can help you stir up your dream. Think about what you want - what you *really want* and why. **Forget what someone else says you should do or have, or the path our culture insists that you follow based on what society deems to be appropriate. Consider the dreams and aspirations that are born from the depths of *your* being.** Those ideas and inspirations will tell you who you were created to be and what you were designed to do.

If you can dream it, you can do it. JUST APPLY POWER
-Walt Disney   PATIENCE
                                            PASSION

I have within me the strength, patience and passion to do it.

WANT TO FILL A DREAM?
POUR IN POWER
PATIENCE
PASSION

Follow-Up After the Follow-Up

It doesn't matter whether you're short of money, people, energy, or time. What God invites you to do will always be greater than the resources you start with.
-Bruce Wilkinson

God wants to partner with us as a limitless resource, to do things we can't do by and as ourselves

After spending several days (what actually felt like weeks) on the couch and in the recliner after undergoing reconstructive surgery to repair a ruptured Achilles tendon, I began questioning whether or not I could write this book. I am a person of action and excitement - I'm always on the go. But while temporarily immobilized, fear and doubt started creeping into my mind. *An idle mind is the devil's workshop!* Amen?

During that time, I recalled a quote from someone who I never had the privilege of meeting, but someone I consider a mentor, the late Zig Ziglar: "You are what you are and where you are because of what's gone into your mind." I felt defeated. I asked myself how in Sam Hill (I literally said that, just in case you were wondering) am I going to write a book? Other questions followed. *Who would actually buy my book? What have I even accomplished? Where am I going to find the resources to pull this off? How would people look at me if I wrote a book and it was a flop?* You name it, it crossed my mind.

Looking for an answer to get over the hump, to revitalize a project that began several months earlier, I revisited Clifton at his home one afternoon after a follow-up appointment with the orthopedic. When I arrived, I met his wife and dog, and en route to the back patio he stopped to grab us a drink (a ginger ale for me - one of my favorites) and he picked up another stack of books. As we talked, he casually shared story after story of the places he has been, the people he has met, and the vast numbers of lives that have been positively impacted by some of the seemingly insignificant decisions that have been made in his life. Do you have people in your life that energize you? They inspire you, nourish you, and bring out the best in you. He's one of them. He didn't know it, but what he shared that day was the very spark I needed.

He recalled the season in which he published his first book (*Ford and the American Dream,* 2007) and the residual footprints it has left halfway around the world. A gentleman called him up to congratulate him on the book - told him that he enjoyed it, but wanted his expert advice on a matter. He asked Clifton if he could refer him to a solid leadership program. He was looking for something to implement with the group of people who worked with him at several car dealerships he owned. Clifton referenced Ken Blanchard's *Lead Like Jesus.* The gentleman didn't ask another question. He expressed his appreciation, hung up the phone and went to work on putting the program in place. After opening up the leadership program to other leaders in the community as well, a lady originally from a country in Africa attended. She caught a vision that day of what this program could do for thousands of people in the area where she was born. John Maxwell says, "Everything rises and falls on leadership."

After traveling home and finding a way to duplicate the program to the best of her ability, she did just that. She reached thousands with the leadership program. It generated such a pleasing response that she received a call from a government official asking if she would share what she had done. The program eventually made it's way into the hands, heads, and hearts of people who had significant power. What was the result? It changed the habits of many. It lead to the amendment of laws of that country.

> *Know that everything will happen at just the right time, at just the right place, with just the right people.*
> -Wayne W. Dyer God's Plan

Clifton's story gave me chill bumps. It's a true testament of what is possible and how one person can be used to affect change if they exercise faith through action. Tony Dungy, NFL coaching great, ties it together nicely by saying, "Don't ever sell yourself short. God's purposes are greater than man's purposes. There is much to do and much that you are capable of doing." Did Clifton ever in his wildest imagination anticipate impacting thousands of lives and the changing of a government somewhere around the globe? Absolutely not. But he did tell me that he faced similar fears in the completion of his first literary work. And what he found out when he decided to run in the direction of those fears is this: they disappeared.

Run at the fear, make them disappear

He affirmed my dream that day. He reminded me, with confidence, "Whatever your dream is, get engaged and follow it.... If you're bold, you'll get out there and do it. **Get up, dress up, show up, and don't give up.** That's all I did. God did the rest. I got in the car; He put the gas in the tank."

Needless to say, I decided to chin up and return to my mission. So, here it is. Enjoy.

*Disclaimer: I am not held responsible for any breakthrough that may occur in your life as a direct result of the application of information that follows. If you choose to become a dreamer and bear arms with greatness, it is due to a decision made from your own heart.

Power
Potential
+ Passion

A Dream Life

Run at the fear
make it disappear
thats what Jesus
DID on the cross
suffering in our eyes
opened up the skies
Releasing Grace and mercy
Though the cost

1

D is for DARE

Dream no small dreams. They have
no power to stir the souls of men.
-Victor Hugo

Do you remember what it was like as a kid when someone dared you to do something? You couldn't back down from a dare! If so, you would get laughed at by all of your friends and called a chicken. How many times did you step up to the challenge because you loved that feeling you got when you were able to prove someone wrong? You know, that swag you had - like Michael Jackson back-in-the-day in his *Bad* video, when you told your peers, "See! I told you I'd do it!" It was fun, wasn't it?

Daredevil

A cousin of mine dared me to do a complete rotation (flip completely over) on a set of multi-colored metal parallel bars on the playground at a park in my hometown. It was an Olympic-like feat, but I accepted the challenge. Myron was bigger, faster and stronger than me, like the rest of my cousins, so I thought this could help me earn some "street cred" with all of them. I was always looking for a way to prove myself, so that one day I would earn first pick honors when teams were being selected to play football or basketball in the neighborhood. So, here was another opportunity.

Dad was hooping with the older guys (who didn't allow me to play at the time because of my size, and that's another story that we don't have time for) not very far from the playground. I jumped up, grabbing both bars with either hand. To gain some momentum, I began rocking back and forth, swinging my feet out in front of me. In that very moment the thought surfaced that we all have when we know we're in the middle of doing something completely stupid - *why am I doing this?* But at the same time, you know that if you pull it off and it goes as planned, you'll be able to change your nickname to "thebomb.com."

As my legs approached the position where I was perpendicular to the ground, it looked as if my feet were going to brush the leaves of the trees. Then... gravity decided to have some fun. I also forgot, since this was my first rodeo, to maneuver my arms in a way that I could rotate over. Plus, it didn't dawn on me until I was on my way down that my arms were actually too short for this stunt.

My three foot nothing frame rotated around with my hands no longer fastened to the bars. I began to fall. It happened so quickly that the only thing I could do was close my eyes, brace myself, and hope that it wasn't God's time to call me home. I don't think I even knew how to pray, but I asked God to forgive me for biting my little sister's pinky finger when she was a baby. It had to be a sin because Mom busted my butt. And then it happened... BOOM! I came crashing to the ground, which was speckled with tiny pebbles, landing flat on my stomach, elbows, palms of my hands, and my chin bounced off the ground. Yeah, it hurt.

I knew it hurt because Myron immediately said it looked like it did. That was a nice observation on his part. But I literally knew it hurt because it felt like Adam Vinatieri kicked a football into my stomach. You know that feeling you get when you get the air knocked out of you? Yeah, that was it.

The story became even more animated as I got up, oblivious to the fact that my chin was gushing blood. Myron would never admit to it, but I think he almost passed out when he saw the blood. Needless to say, Old Man D's basketball game was interrupted and I was rushed to the hospital to get stitched up.

It's fun to look back and remember that moment, and many moons later I have a pretty cool scar to show for my bravery. I've always been told that chicks dig scars. It's also served as a conversation piece on many occasions. But here's the point I want you to get: when you were young, you were just like me; you were a daredevil. You were a superhero. You were ambitious. You wanted to rule the world. You wanted to be a pilot, astronaut, veterinarian, baseball player or fire fighter. And when someone dared you to do something, you didn't hesitate, you just did it. Often times, it didn't even take a dare in order to do something crazy. Maybe you had the same intestinal fortitude that Squints had when he sacrificed his well-being at the pool for the likes of Wendy Peffercorn one hot summer day (*The Sandlot*, 1993). Why is it, however, that as you get older the opposite is true?

As adults, people no longer dare you to do things; they actually plead for you *not to*. Do people forget how to be curious and ambitious? Is it that people are paralyzed by the thought of the pain of disappointment of past efforts not working in what they would consider their favor? Once upon a time, we were embarrassed and even scolded by others for not doing something outside the box. Now, we're actually scorned for doing the very things that most people are scared to do - dream, take risks, do something others are unfamiliar with.

I'm sure you can relate to my silly attempt at park gymnastics, because I failed miserably. What mattered most was I tried. I didn't back down. Although I nearly met my Maker that day, I literally and figuratively picked myself up off the ground since it didn't kill me. I wish I would've been introduced to one of my mentors, Les Brown, a lot sooner. I would've taken his advice: "When you fall, try landing on your back, because if you can look up you can get up."

> *The race will go to the curious, the slightly mad, and those with an unsatiated passion for learning and dare deviltry.*
> -Tom Peters

Wake-up Call

Although it wasn't a traditional dare as I just described, I received an invitation to step out of the muck and mire of the mundane when I witnessed something special happen for a friend of mine. Like most people, I was cruising along doing what I had always done. I played basketball my whole life, I loved helping people and I had a deep appreciation for the teachers and coaches I had growing up. So, it seemed fitting, a no-brainer even, to be a teacher and coach.

With very little responsibility at the age of 27 - no wife, no children, no mortgage and no student loans - the meager salary of a public school teacher allowed me to get by. Based on my circumstances, I felt I had no reason to grow. A couple of years doing what I was doing and things had become monotonous. **I was planning on doing tomorrow what I had done yesterday and I was no closer to the goals that I did not have.** The reality was this: I wasn't going to be any better (at anything) tomorrow than I was yesterday because I was two days older. But when I found out how a friend of mine named Jason went from "zero to hero" in what seemed like overnight, my mind took the first step down a different path. That first step turned into an all-out sprint to become the very best version of me (something I work on every single day). I began to dream.

Have I piqued your interest, yet? Let me explain what I mean by "zero to hero." In no way, shape, form or fashion am I saying Jason *was* a zero. What I'm saying is he, like most people, and myself, was living a life of quiet desperation only to eventually arrive safely at his grave. Consider two of those words for a moment - *quiet* and *safely*. Jason once said: **"Most people have been going down the road to nowhere because they've been told that it's safe there."** He was spinning his wheels financially, living paycheck to paycheck, going nowhere fast. And guess what? **If you don't know where you're going, any road will take you there.**

Jason's incredible success story made me feel very uncomfortable about the lot I had settled for early in life. Better yet, it inspired me. It gave me hope. It moved me to action. Let's backtrack a bit and I'll fill in the gaps.

We're Gonna Have to Let You Go

Jason Keltner and I were high school acquaintances and track teammates. That would change during college, as we became roommates and friends sharing a living space in the summer one block from my college campus in our hometown of Campbellsville, Kentucky.

After wrapping up our education degrees and entering the wide world of teaching, we quickly found ourselves in a bind. Our backs were against the wall as state employees because of budget cuts. Jason was then introduced to a turnkey business model by a fellow teacher, Chris Estes (author of *The A.P.P.L.E. Principle,* 2013), with a network marketing company that manufactures and distributes first-to-market health and wellness products. It was an opportunity to start at the bottom and work his way to the top based on how hard he worked. Jason shared the same opportunity with me and two days later, in 2008, I was the first person to join him in business. We became "Independent Business Owners." Nevermind the fact that I overdrew my checking account to get started.

The following spring after my little-big brother, Michael, graduated high school, and Jessica, my beautiful younger sister, already had her feet wet in college, I packed my bags and relocated. I accepted a head coaching position of a girl's basketball team at the varsity level at a high school in Vette City, USA - Bowling Green, Kentucky. Little did I know, the next two and a half years would rock my world, because I *didn't do* what Jason *chose to do*. I stopped building our business consistently and correctly.

From 2008 to 2010, each year Jason was told his teaching position would be cut. He was "pink-slipped" (written notification that you no longer have a staffed position at a school) three consecutive years. He then decided to hang up teaching. **He quit his day job, but he didn't quit on his day dream.** What happened for Jason in less than half a decade (less time than it took him to complete his undergraduate degree and receive his teaching certificate) would become one of the most celebrated stories of our company.

Part-time, from home, he replaced not only his salary, but his wife's salary along with his mother's. They were able to fire their boss and walk away from traditional employment. Jason began participating in mission trips *and* funding them. He started his own non-profit disaster relief organization and volunteered his time to teach Physical Education and develop a championship archery team at a Christian school in our community. I saw his lifestyle completely change. I saw him growing. It was at that time, in 2011, that I realized he and his family were earning in most months what I was earning in a year as a full-time teacher and coach. And here's the kicker: it was residual - meaning he had created a substantial six-figure income and would continue to get paid whether he left home or not. That got my attention. Another thing that got my attention was a quote I read from Jim Rohn: "The book you don't read won't help." So, I opened a book that had been collecting dust in my bedroom, *Rich Dad, Poor Dad*, by Robert Kiyosaki. I found out only a couple of pages in that the "Rich Dad" owned a business and the "Poor Dad" was a teacher.

Jason was married to his wife and not his job. I noticed that he could spend as much time as he wanted to with his daughter (now two daughters) and he didn't have to ask his boss to take off work in order to do so. I noticed that he had something else that you can't put a price tag on and that's peace of mind. I noticed he was building his dream instead of working 40-plus hours a week building someone else's dream. I noticed he had the time freedom and financial security to give of himself and his resources to the causes that he felt compelled to support, based on where God was calling him. I noticed he had a growing confidence. Are you picking up what I'm putting down here? He had what I wanted!

The Light Bulb Came On

It was in that "A-ha!" moment that I made the shift. The light bulb came on for me. With Jason's ability to commit to a process, follow his dream, and see it through, he became the first individual that I truly knew to have massive success in network marketing. Technically there were a couple of other people, like Estes, who had also seen success, but I connected with Jason because we came from the same place. He was a good 'ole boy from the Bluegrass State who walked the halls of the same schools as me. **I knew that if he could do it, I could do it.**

Have you ever heard the story of a guy by the name of John Newton? He began his career at sea working slave ships, then became a prominent supporter of abolitionism. How did such a turnaround happen? It happened in the midst of a storm, literally and figuratively. It was such a profound conversion that he was spiritually prompted to write the words of what most people would consider the world's most recognizable and moving hymn, *Amazing Grace*.

I once was lost, but now I'm found. Was blind, but now I see…

-Amazing Grace

Although his newfound religious conviction, at the time, prompted him to move toward God, what most people don't know is that he worked actively in the slave trade even after his initial exposure to God. Jason Pettus, Senior Pastor at Living Hope Baptist Church (Bowling Green, Kentucky), commented on Newton during a Sunday worship service by saying: "He continued to sell slaves after his initial experience with God… But once God got ahold of his heart, he became a maverick and a leader like no other!"

Like Newton, everything from the point of my awakening, if you will, wasn't necessarily sunshine, rainbows and yellow brick roads. I can't say every decision was the right decision, but I can say that I decided to move in a different direction. I could hear something calling my name. I could feel something tugging my heart.

What I realized in that critical moment was how important it was that Jason had gone before me and made it happen. **See, the first step toward greatness for many people is taken when they see someone else *living their own dream.*** My reality immediately changed because my thoughts surrounding what was possible changed. Ask the scores of people who followed Roger Bannister's footsteps in conquering the infamous four-minute mile barrier if his 3:59.4 date with destiny on May 6, 1954 changed their perspective a bit. And If you can change your thoughts, you can change your world. Jason helped me toss my old script in the trash, and as the director of my play, rewriting my agreement with reality allowed me to reinvent myself.

33

Change is Necessary

Most people accept their circumstances not knowing they harbor the power to create their destiny. We are all living in the residual of our past thoughts and expectations. That residual for me was broke, busted and disgusted. I was actually so broke I had a dream one time that I pulled up to the ATM to get some cash, and when I rolled down my window, the alarm in the bank went off! In the same dream, I drove home to pull up my account online and on a full battery my laptop shut down when I entered my login and password! When I accepted the truth that I had not only the ability, but the God-given right to change where I was at, I got lost in my dream because it became so big. James Allen wrote: "The soul will attract that which it secretly harbors." I gave myself permission to respect where I was at, but change where I was going. You can, too.

Myron Golden says in one of his books: "I believe that people who are financially challenged should not watch television until they are financially free." I also recall someone telling me once upon a time that if someone else's stack (money) was bigger than yours you should listen to them. So, with my checking account overdrawn and more month left at the end of the money, I cancelled my cable, sold my TV and sold my golf clubs. This gave me cash capital to reinvest in my business. It also gave me some leeway to start working on my dream versus watching others living out theirs while mine went "down the tube." It also allowed me to start working on *me*. Per the recommendation of some folks I highly respect, I stuck my nose in a few good books and went to work on developing myself.

The average person may feel like that was a radical move. Yeah, it was. I wanted radical change. What about you? Have you come to the place in the road where you've realized that if you keep doing what you've been doing, you'll keep getting what you've been getting? It's time to be bold! Change is necessary!

Life is either a daring adventure or nothing.
-Helen Keller

* * * * *

Some people never experience their dream or fulfill their destiny because they never dare to step outside of their mental cubicle. If you don't have a dream, how can you have a dream come true? When was the last time you did something for the first time? When was the last time you did something that scares you?

You can either go to work building your dream or end up working for someone who did build theirs. The choice is yours. Those who dare, do; those who dare not, do not. **If you want something you've never had before, it's time to do something you've never done before.** Go ahead; do it! I dare you!

Dare Notes

_____

_____

_____

_____

_____

_____

_____

_____

_____

_____

_____

_____

_____

_____

_____

_____

_____

_____

D.R.E.A.M.

2

R is for RISK

Two roads diverged in a wood, and I - I took the one less traveled by, and that has made all the difference.

-Robert Frost

A wise man once told me to steer clear of the "good opinion" of other people. He meant that people will always tell you what you should or shouldn't do and what they think is best for you. His point has held true for me. As I began growing my business with a freakishly laser-like focus and unmatched sense of urgency, the people in my life gladly (not always kindly) shared their stance on my mission. It'll happen to you, too. Prepare yourself now by accepting the fact that the road less traveled is filled with opposition brilliantly disguised as opportunity. Risk takers value freedom over safety. Plenty people had plenty to say about me, but I was so lost in my pursuit that much of it sounded like Charlie Brown's teacher: "Wah, wah, wah, wah, wah..."

Psychologically Unemployable

My excitement grew as I grew my business. The more successful people I studied and the more I fed my faith, the more I starved my fear and increased my vision. I read books like *Think & Grow Rich* (Hill, 2005), *How to Win Friends & Influence People* (Carnegie, 1998), *Twelve Pillars* (Rohn & Widener, 2011) ... and listened to audio CDs like

As A Man Thinketh (Allen, 2013), *Born to Win* (Ziglar, 2012), *10 Secrets for Success and Inner Peace* (Dyer, 2002). As I became more self-confident, this crazy idea surfaced to quit my full-time teaching and coaching job. Although I will admit I was far from ready, it was like I had developed a mindset that was "psychologically unemployable." And what's *ready* mean, anyway? My mind had been stretched and it certainly wasn't going back to where it once was. I knew that taking this step would be tough - an uphill battle. But I was inspired and I knew in the future I didn't want anyone writing my checks but *me*.

> *Don't wait until everything is just right. It will never be perfect. There will always be challenges, obstacles, and less than perfect conditions. So what. Get started now. With each step you take, you will grow stronger and stronger, more and more skilled, more and more self-confident, and more and more successful.*
> -Mark Victor Hansen

Maybe this was a mistake; maybe it wasn't, so I started sharing my newly formulated plans with a few people around me. How do you think they responded? Yep. And those voices grew pretty loud. I was told things like: *"Are you seriously considering walking away from all these benefits?" "Jeremy, whatever you do, do not quit your day job!" "Are you crazy? Dude, you have summers off - you've got it made!" "You went to school to get a degree that you're not even gonna use?" "Do you really think you can make it in one of those things? I've seen some people get in one and it didn't turn out very good."*

There were a few wisecracks and naysayers who came crawling out of the woodwork (like "Haterade" was on sale,

10 for 10 at Kroger). Just as society attempts to demoralize our daring to dream, the same applies when we take risks. Everyone wants us to play it safe, to be careful, to not get our hopes up. Most will say it's because they don't want you to do something out of the ordinary, and when it doesn't work out, have to see you disappointed and let down. It's all about you, right? Your best interest. But what most people don't know is that for people like me (and hopefully you) the pain of regret hurts more if the shot isn't taken. I was tired of merely existing. Something inside me burned for more. And therein lies an important lesson I learned: **You don't need anyone to approve your dream. It wasn't given to them; it was given to you.** Although I respected the opinions of others, I had no desire to be a "King of the Comfort Zone." Someone else could gladly apply for that position. Daring to dream gave me an itch and the only way to scratch it was to do something big.

> *. . . lion chasers are more afraid of lifelong regrets than temporary uncertainty.*
> *-Mark Batterson*

If They Wouldn't Cry, You Shouldn't Care

Around this time I can recall a great book, now a mentor and friend, Chris Estes, recommended: *The Slight Edge.* In that book, Jeff Olson shares a story of a tipping point he has that coincides with what I'm trying to get across here. Early in his career in the corporate world he knew that successful people were simply willing to do what unsuccessful people weren't. He, too, faced opposition and fear. While praying for clarity and confidence over his first sales call, his answer came in the form of an article in a magazine. The article said that at the average funeral about ten people cry. It went on to say that the number one factor that determined who would transition from the funeral procession to the burial was the weather. It read that if rain was coming down, fifty percent of the people who attended your funeral would checkout and ditch the burial.

Jeff's take goes like this:

You know what? I don't give a damn what anybody thinks of what I'm doing any more. If the odds are that iffy as to whether or not they even cry at my funeral, and chances are fifty-fifty that they duck out before I'm planted if the sky happens to cry for me more than the people do ... then why am I spending so much time worrying about what they're thinking now?

I don't know about you, but when I read that for the first time I nearly dropped down and started repping push-ups because I was so fired up. As a matter of fact, referencing it in this book may have fired me up even more. Let me ask you this: Why should you and I be afraid of rejection? Why should we be worried about what the 95 Percent say? **The road to the "Land of Average" was paved by the masses.** And that's not where I'm headed and neither are you if I have anything to do with it.

Dreamers have a different agenda. Dreamers are daredevils and risk-takers. Dreamers don't go where the path may lead; they go where there is none and leave a trail. Dreamers are people who are willing to live uncomfortably, temporarily, in order to attain a life that is genuinely comfortable. **Dreamers find out what other people are doing and they do the opposite.**

Where's Your Beach?

While building my business I had the opportunity to reconnect with a college teammate who resides in Panama City, Florida, which this allowed me to open a new market there. I traveled south to support the growing market several times during the spring and summer of 2011. That's not a bad deal, huh? Building a business at the beach certainly has its perks. It was exciting, to say the least. I was so excited about it that I actually cashed in a couple of sick days at work to travel there on a Thursday (Shhh! Don't tell on me!), presented and trained for my team through that Sunday, and made it back home (nine hour drive) at 2:00 a.m. Monday morning. I was at work bright eyed and bushy tailed at 7:00 a.m.

While in the Sunshine State, I would hit the beach, enjoy the sun and the sand, read and reflect, make a friend and meet their friends, and in the evening share story after story from living room to living room.

One trip played host to a huge change in my life. I received a phone call from my girlfriend of nearly six years, literally moments after pulling into Panama City, with news that our relationship was ending effective immediately. Caroline (my sweet Corolla) and I drove all the way home to confront the situation, then we drove all the way back down honoring my commitment to help the team a day later. That's over 1,600 miles in 72 hours. Jim Rohn and Wayne Dyer spoke to my heart from the speakers of my car during "Drive Time University." It was an Independence Day weekend (no pun intended) that I'll never forget.

It was the very next trip to that same beach that *I decided* to make a huge change in my life. I resigned from my head coaching position. I drew my phone from the cup holder of my beach chair one morning, dialed one of my assistant principals, informed him and asked what was the next step in the process. I ended the call, and right there from my phone, opened my email and typed my letter of resignation. It was frightening, but it was also liberating.

If you never make the attempt, you may never know the depths of despair, but neither will you experience the exhilaration of success.
-Napoleon Hill

No More Lesson Plans

As the 2011-2012 school year began, out of respect for my employer, I let it be known that there was a strong chance that this would be my last year as a teacher in the public school system. I knew I would revisit with the administration before the end of the fall semester. When winter rolled around, with two weeks left in the semester, I decided there would be no more lesson plans. Have you ever seen the movie *Major Payne*? It's one of my favorite throwback comedies. There's a scene where one of Major Payne's comrades is injured in battle. Payne arrives on the scene and asks, "Want me to show you a little trick - take your mind off that arm?" With his best interest at heart, he affectionately breaks the guys finger to distract him from the pain of a gunshot wound. Walking away from coaching didn't seem so scary once I submitted my resignation from teaching, which is what paid the bills and put food on the table and clothes on my back.

When someone asked master motivator Eric Thomas if he had a safety net after he quit his "9 to 5," he replied, "Yes, I have three safety nets: hustle, heart, and faith." Although I was a bit uneasy, I knew that the only true way to grow was to get comfortable with being uncomfortable. Everything we want, any great success, and all dreams come true just outside of our comfort zone. How do I know this? It's modeled for us by the Les Browns of the world, who had no place to live and washed up in a public restroom, on his way to public speaking stardom. It's modeled for us by people like the Wright Brothers, Orville and Wilbur, who said: "If we worked on the assumption that what is accepted as true really is true, then there would be little hope for advance." It's modeled for us by Thomas Edison, who was out of his mind just enough to serve up 1,093 patents for inventions while battling diabetes, stomach ailments and deafness. It's also modeled for us by Colonel Sanders, who traveled the country after the age of 65, refusing to accept a meager retirement after a meager social security check and accepted over a thousand nos before someone decided his fried chicken recipe was good enough.

> *Life begins at the end of your comfort zone.*
> -Neale Donald Walsch

If you're a dreamer like me, you've got something brewing in your heart and you don't go for it, what's the alternative? Or better yet, here's another question: What's the worst that can happen? The reality is that everything is risky. If you want to avoid all risk, then it's simple, don't do anything at all. The next time you need to hit the grocery store, don't go. Stay at home. Automobiles contribute to approximately 20 percent of all fatal accidents. The next time you feel like stepping outside to go for a brisk walk and get some fresh air, don't do it. That's how upwards of 15 percent of all accidents occur. Is it safe to stay at home? Accidents even happen there. Helen Keller once said: "Avoiding danger is no safer in the long run than outright exposure." Couple that with Mark Twain's timeless message: "Twenty years from now you will be more disappointed by the things you didn't do than by the things you did do." Both of those individuals lived a life that encourages us to sail away from the safe harbor and discover what we're made of. Risk is *necessary*.

Sure, letting go of my primary income was a concern. Discontinuing certain benefits for a brief stint wasn't necessarily the smartest thing to do, in eyes of some people. The fear of possibly returning to teaching a year or two later because it didn't work out made my stomach churn. But none of those factors weighed heavier than the fear of what I would miss out on if I didn't go for it. At the core of my being I knew I was a champion and champions are bold.

> *Life is inherently risky. There is only one big risk you should avoid at all costs, and that is the risk of doing nothing.*
> -Denis Waitley

It's All A Matter of Perspective

What if you began looking at obstacles differently too? What if you decided to adopt a different philosophy? The bigger the risk, the bigger the reward. What if right now you chose to believe that failure is actually doing nothing at all? How would that impact your dream? Would it raise the bar? Would it take the lid off?

Most people concern themselves with, *"What if it doesn't work?"* Are you like most people? If so, that's okay, but I'm not. And I have a pretty good feeling that you're not, either - you picked up this book to better yourself. If you're anything like the people I hang out with, you say, *"What if it does work?"* Of course leaving the friendly confines of everything you know poses a threat. It is dangerous. But if you don't go, you'll never grow. That's a fact.

I believe God doesn't call you to do something or place a work in your heart unless He plans on equipping you with exactly what you need to complete the mission. Take Jason Brown, former pro football standout, for example; once upon a time he had a five-year, $37 million contract with the St. Louis Rams. He gave it all up to farm (First Fruits Farm) - something he had never done before! He confessed to learning how to farm by watching YouTube videos!

> *. . . when I think about a life of greatness, I think about a life of service.*
> -Jason Brown

Taking risks requires faith and faith embraces uncertainty. Those who go on to accomplish big things and influence a lot of people, step out into the darkness. They're guided by the light of their faith and the internal compass of their dream. Until you do what you've never done, you'll never discover what else you can do. **Until you challenge what is impossible, you'll never uncover what is possible for you.**

Highly successful leaders ignore conventional wisdom and take chances. Their stories inevitably include a defining moment or key decision when they took a significant risk and thereby experienced a breakthrough.
-Larry Osborne

Back to the Basics

Taking risks also requires guts. Consider what happened to a close friend of mine, Mark Alderson. Mark knew the end of his story, because he's a champion. However, he lost focus and got away from the fundamentals for a season of his life. Mark checked out on a dream during the Christmas break of his freshman year in college. Looking for his lot in life, trying to find his place while disgruntled with his circumstances, he veered from the path he was on.

After dabbling in construction, working at a factory here and there, getting his barber's license and even bouncing at night clubs (security detail), just to get by, he decided to draw a line in the sand. "The road I was on was leading to a dead end," Mark described. He hit the turning signal on his way home from work one afternoon, pulled to the side of the road and made a single phone call that would change the trajectory of his life. Mark decided to return to college, finish his degree and play out the rest of his basketball eligibility, six years later. Why did he do it? Because that still, small voice inside of him wouldn't allow him to retire to bed another night accepting that *someday* he could be *somebody.* In order for things to change, we have to change. And Mark knew *that* someday would never come and *that* somebody would never show up unless he made a change.

Originally planning to attend a different college (another one that recruited him out of high school), he ran into our coaches (one of whom was an assistant on the staff when Mark decided to pull his Ricky Williams disappearing act) at a fast-food joint when he traveled to Campbellsville to fetch his transcript. Their conversation that day led Mark to return to Campbellsville University.

What was Mark's mission? He wanted to finish what he started and become the first person in his immediate family to earn a college degree. I didn't know it that day when he stepped into Powell Athletic Center dressed in street clothes during a practice in 2004, but he would become a pivotal part of our program's success over the next two years. The by-product of that was he would become a lifelong friend, even a "big brother."

What makes Mark's story special? The risk. He made a u-turn when most people would've kept on doing what they were doing, getting what they were getting. With the support of his parents, Mark put some financial obligations on hold. That raised the eyebrows of a few of his family members. Another concern his family had was the fact that he had a few extra miles under his belt – he was much older at this point. He was laughed at by many of his peers. He certainly wasn't in the playing shape that he was at the age of 18 or 19.

In response to the opposition and fear of failing, Mark moved forward. That's what winners do. That's what dreamers do. The conference title and trip to the NAIA Division I Sweet Sixteen our senior year, coupled with graduation, was worth it. He also received a phone call one day while we were in our dorm room with a report that a buddy from his previous circle of influence had been mugged and stabbed: "a walking autopsy with 800 staples holding his body together," Mark recalls.

> *I could've been a champion in that life, but you have to be brave enough to change your environment if you want to change your world.*
> -Mark Alderson

Wouldn't you agree with me that his decision to course correct and take a risk was worth it? Instead of accepting his circumstances, Mark decided to create his destiny. Significant achievements have never been obtained by taking small risks with small things. Mark now has two degrees; one of those being from "Hard Knock University." He's a successful entrepreneur, married to the love of his life and owns a lovely homestead. He knows that **if you're not growing, you're dying, and if you're not risking anything, you're losing everything**. And if you want the sharpest fade in America, go check him out. He's the guy with the beard on the by-pass in Bowling Green.

* * * * *

Some people never experience their dream or fulfill their destiny because fear fogs their memory, clouds their vision and creates confusion, paralyzing their ability to move. Timid people who tip-toe around don't get promoted. **Your greatest gains and biggest breakthroughs in this life will happen when you start taking risks regularly.**

Risks require courage. Unfortunately, that's something most people don't have. It's impossible to achieve anything great without a great risk. Speaking of impossible, let's just go ahead and remove that from our vocabulary. Let's just tear it out of our dictionaries! We may end up throwing a few other "i" words in the trash with it, but I think we'll get along just fine.

If you take risks and fail, you will have fewer regrets than if you did nothing at all. **Destroy your limiting beliefs about what can and can't happen or what will or won't work.** If you never get out of the boat, you'll never walk on water. Infinite possibilities are waiting for you! Go for it! Risk away!

Risk Notes

_____

_____

_____

_____

_____

_____

_____

_____

_____

_____

_____

_____

_____

_____

_____

_____

_____

_____

D.R.E.A.M.

3

E is for EXCITEMENT

The most challenging thing you'll ever face in your life is learning every day to be excited about what you're doing.
-Charles Jones

Do you, by chance, disagree with Charles' quote up there? I didn't think you did. It's safe to say work (hard work) is tiring, frustrating and monotonous. Darren Hardy, publisher of *SUCCESS* Magazine, says success is "hard freakin' work." Guess what my dream requires? Hard freakin' work! Guess what your dream requires? Hard freakin' work! So it's wise to respect the opinions of super achievers like Hardy and Art Williams, who transitioned from coaching to business - similar to myself, believes that it's easy to stay excited for a day, a week, a month, and maybe even a couple of years. But what's hard is staying excited long enough until the job gets done. The most common cause of an unfulfilled dream is quitting. Excitement moves people to action, but it's fueling that fire on a daily basis that leads to success and the manifestation of a dream.

Keep Your Head Up

While growing up, my dad always reminded me in everything I did and in everything I went through to stay positive and to keep my head up. He was humbled by his beginnings, being one of ten children in his family, eight of them being sisters (yikes!). He taught me how to be a *Philippians 4:11-13* man and how to appreciate what The Bible says in *Romans 8:28.* When I questioned whether or not I wanted to continue playing college ball after a dismal freshman year, he reminded me that tough times come and go, but tough people last. That pain may shack up for the night, but joy comes in the morning. Through two divorces, walking countless miles to and from work, paying child support many, many years, holding down two jobs, picking up odds and ends work here and there, going some days without much food, he was the most positive person I knew. He has a rich soul and would gladly volunteer to give anyone the shirt off his back, even in a storm.

Like most women, my mother took a firm stance on some things. One of those things was me getting back up when I had been knocked down. She gave me an earful after a game early in my playing career. It was basically tough love, but it was an earful. I took a hard hit while chasing after a loose ball and I didn't hustle to my feet after coming up short - a combination of disappointment and fatigue. Regardless of the reason, she didn't take to it well, and her child WAS NOT going to mope around on the floor, pouting and sulking! It was a hard lesson from her that if I was going to "lay down" when I got knocked down, then she wasn't going to waste her time, energy and money putting me on a platform to play. I either played like a winner, or I didn't play at all. I respected her position because she learned how to be tough after giving birth to me when she was only 18 years old. I'm sure that was scary, but she made it work.

What they both taught me, in a nutshell, early in life, is that to achieve a dream you must pay a price. Part of that fee is moving from failure to failure without loss of enthusiasm.

If you have a dream, you protect it from encroaching outside forces by staying excited.

Nice Shirt

After I got serious about my dream, I met a guy named Brandon Hayes. He had on a tee shirt that read *YOUNG AND FREE*. It piqued my interest, so I inquired. If you know Brandon, then you know not to ask him certain questions, because you'll end up learning a lot more than you wanted to (he can get pretty long winded). On this particular subject, he had a philosophy and a vision that aligned with how I felt about attitude, personal development, education, goals and dreams. He didn't realize it, but before I even considered it a viable option to leave teaching and coaching, he sold me a ticket for a 52-week vacation.

He hardly took a breath as he articulated that most people are walking around on a daily basis negative, dull and disillusioned - whining, crying and complaining about their situations and circumstances - sucking their thumbs. He continued, "Most people lack passion and have no fire in their belly because they don't know what they're designed to do and they don't know what they're capable of achieving."

Brandon rounded third and brought it home by sharing with me that he once upon a time worked an 80-hour work week. "I was a slave to my J-O-B!," he explained. And he, like everyone else, had a choice to either keep standing on the sideline or raise the lid from his thinking and get busy pursuing something bigger.

I could tell that Brandon was enthralled by his dream. He was consumed by the idea of showing people a better way to live. Technically, I was already doing what he was doing. But if I wasn't, I would have joined him on the spot. He had me ready to run through a brick wall as he painted a picture with words of what life could look like if you had health, time, and money - all three at the same time; that you could go where you wanted, when you wanted and with whom you wanted, just because you wanted.

When you get that excited, passion seeps from your pores. You become a magnet. People are drawn to you. You also become a tool that God uses to express life through. You can raise everyone else's level of play. You make everyone around you better. Brandon made me better. And eight months after that conversation, he traveled to school to visit with me on my final day as a teacher. When he called to ask if he could stop by, I insisted that he not waste his time making the trip. He disregarded my request, stating, "Today, we set another captive free! I wouldn't dare miss this!"

His trip to school that day set a friendship in motion. We've now celebrated birthdays in Vegas, enjoyed mangled up waffles in Chicago (made by yours truly, from a hotel breakfast bar), flown into the wrong airport in Orlando, even skied and face planted on the hills of the Smokies in Gatlinburg. But the best of all has been the countless late nights invested in sharing ideas and building dreams that most people would laugh at because they're so big.

> *Surround yourself with positive people and situations, and avoid negativity.*
> -Doreen Virtue

Mr. Excitement

This particular puzzle piece of the *D.R.E.A.M.* acronym happens to be nearest and dearest to my heart. Is it any more important than the rest? Not necessarily. But it's been the secret ingredient to my success. I'm sure my level of excitement has rubbed some people the wrong way, but I learned to stop worrying about that a long time ago.

You have to get this settled right now: if you're going to bring an unparalleled excitement to the game each day, people are going to look at you funny. They're going to mock you. They're going to say some inappropriate things. But what I have heard said about success, the same can be applied to excitement: the only taste of excitement some people will ever have is the bite they *try* to take out of yours.

I was always the emotional leader on the hardwood. I was the crazy-cool teacher who didn't mind acting like a complete idiot in front of the entire school at a pep rally. Some people feel as if I have some kind of predisposition to being more excited, more positive or happier than most people. I don't know if that's the case. I have no idea if that's even possible, to be quite frank. I do know, however, that on my journey, excitement has acted like a magnet, attracting the tools and resources, circumstances and people, which I've needed in order to see my dream begin to actualize. My burning desire is the one tool in my tool belt, so to speak, that has never let me down. It's become part of my identity. I didn't have any influence, time, money or special skills when I started dreaming and decided to take, what was at the time, the biggest risk of my life; but I did have energy and excitement. My excitement helped me acquire an abundance mindset. **My excitement helped me**

exercise the genius inside of me that's in all of us - the one that says ANYTHING IS POSSIBLE.

> *Sometimes you have to make up your mind to be excited, and even act excited, until you can become excited.*
> -Clifton Lambreth

Let's get something straight about my philosophy on being excited, though. Yes, I believe in seeing yourself as you already *are* what you would like to *become*. Yes, I believe in speaking life over yourself with positive affirmations. Thoughts become things and words become ways. But I do not believe in "faking it until you make it." If you have a great dream, it's going to take time to accomplish and a team of people to assist. And no one wants to waste their precious time working with someone who isn't genuine, real and honest. If you have to fake it, there's a good chance you're doing something you're not supposed to be doing.

If you are doing what you're supposed to be doing, then you've probably heard this: "If you're doing what you love and loving what you do, you'll never work a day in your life." That's exactly what building the business has felt like for me. I've been more alive than ever before because my work gives me energy; it gives me meaning. I've had the blessing and pleasure of building relationships with people from all parts of the world.

You have to find your passion and your purpose. When you do that, staying excited can, in a sense, become second nature for you. Tony Dungy, in reference to his brother becoming a dentist instead of a football player, said: "His potential was not in following in my footsteps, fulfilling his teachers' expectations, or in any well-worn path in our family. It was in following the passion God had given him and pursuing the joy God had put in front of him. He continues to fulfill his purpose simply by being himself."

You have a dream to follow, a passion to pursue and a calling to recognize. You can't stay excited about that if you're following someone else's path.

Excitement is...

I do all things in my life with this motto: *"If you're not having fun, you're not doing it right!"* Here are five basic ideas, or core values, that have helped me transition from an employee to an entrepreneur. They have helped me grow myself on a daily basis as I've built my dream.

1. Excitement begins with an Attitude of Gratitude

It is impossible to be excited if you're not genuinely grateful for who you are and what you have. Most people waste precious time each day whining and complaining about the person who they are *not* and the things they do *not* have. It's been cited for countless decades by many of the world's greatest thinkers and achievers that what you think about you bring about and what you focus on expands. The more you dwell on what you don't want, the more of what you don't want will continue to show up in your life. Wake up each day and give thanks for what you *do* have. Even if you don't have much, you still have more than most.

Count your blessings. A grateful heart attracts more joy, love, and prosperity.
-Cheryl Richardson

2. Excitement is a choice

While pursuing your dream, this I know for sure; there will be "character building days." No matter how difficult the days ahead may get or how demanding the obstacles may become, there are millions of people who face greater odds. The key to beating your odds is not in changing your circumstances. It's in changing your perspective on your circumstances. It's in changing you. It's a choice. And whether you choose to or choose not to, there will be a consequence.

3. Excitement is caught, not taught

One of my good buddies, Darel Carrier, reminds me often that you can't soar with the eagles if you're pecking around with the chickens. You become what you hang around. Hang out with winners and you'll be a winner. If you want to stay excited, get around other Dream Givers, Problem Solvers, Lid Lifters, Change Agents and Hope Builders - people who have a zest for life. Their excitement, passion and creativity will inspire and encourage you. They'll always have a new idea, something positive to say, something fresh to share.

People are attracted to people who exude confidence and excitement.
-Brandon Hayes

4. Excitement changes your perspective on failure

Lloyd Ogilvie, former Chaplain of the United States Senate, hits the nail right on the head by referencing the positive perspective of a circus performer (flying trapeze): "Once you know that the net below will catch you, you stop worrying about falling. You learn to fall successfully." Excitement teaches you how to turn failure into your best friend. It helps you discipline your disappointments. It helps you turn your failure into stepping stones instead of allowing it to be your gravestone. It even helps you fail faster. If you're not failing, you're not trying. One thing that I have learned along my way is that some of the biggest dreamers are also some of the biggest flops.

5. Excitement creates urgency

In order to achieve your dream and manifest your destiny, it takes a DO IT NOW initiative. Procrastination is a deadly disease. It camps out in graveyards all across the world and invites people to their final resting place with their dreams and desires unmet. But excitement is its arch enemy. Excitement keeps you on the balls of your feet, in anticipation, ready to leap at the next opportunity to do more, be more and achieve more.

A sense of urgency in your work informs you that yesterday is gone forever and tomorrow may never come, but today is in your hands.
-Charles Jones

I knew that in taking a great risk and leaving my job there would be speed bumps, potholes, roadblocks and detours. Chris Estes calls them pop quizzes. But I also knew that if I committed to a process and stayed excited long enough, there would be a great reward.

My passion for learning, growing and building was contagious and it still is today. I want to infect as many people as possible. I want to start a revolution! **Can you imagine a global crusade of excited dreamers rebelliously charging in the direction of greatness? I can see it now... I'd be willing to bet that it would change hearts, businesses, homes, churches, towns, schools and marriages.**

> *Nothing great was ever achieved without enthusiasm.*
> -Ralph Waldo Emerson

Tasha's Toughness

When you are following your heart, pursuing your dream and becoming the person you were designed to be, excitement acts like an inner candle flame. The worst may go before you and the winds of challenge will blow. The flame will flicker at times, but if you are determined it will never blow out.

Tasha Eizinger's flame burns brighter than most. She exemplifies what someone can overcome when they decide to dig in instead of give in. Her story includes a treacherous road she traveled to win her health back. It was a painstaking process, but it was her excitement and childlike faith that kept her moving forward.

Not long ago, Tasha was teaching at an inner city parochial school, on some days from a wheelchair. Her health had declined significantly. Many issues had surfaced, but at the very root of the problem, her body wasn't able to absorb and digest food. In other words, she was basically starving for nutrition, but she didn't know how or why.

She prayed and prayed some more and prayed a little bit more. After multiple attempts to find the cause of her failing health, and no answer, her patience and faith were wearing thin. Words can't describe the frustration that surfaced - young, newly married, highly competitive athlete and only a couple of years into her teaching career. As hope dwindled, she began rationalizing what her life would look like if she accepted these lowly terms and conditions.

Family members recommended a product that provides the most efficacious nutrition found on the planet. Willing to try anything, she gave it a shot and quickly started to see results. As she gained her strength back she began putting her body to the test, eventually completing a Half Ironman (1.2-mile swim, 56-mile bike ride, 13.1-mile run). But it wasn't until she finished that test that she found out her body was battling two parasites and only absorbing 30 percent of the nutrition that she was getting. Tasha developed severe food allergies as well. She was placed on a very strict diet because she was literally fighting for her life. I had no idea just how challenging each day was for her until I flew into Fort Lauderdale, Florida, to assist her and her team with some presentations and new business prospects.

It was a cool late April evening, the sun was down and there had been some rain earlier that afternoon. We walked across the road, from the condo to the sand to visit with the ocean on Deerfield Beach. The waves were coming in under the moonlit Atlantic Ocean sky. Tasha kicked off her sandals, tossed her jacket and darted for the water. Right about the time she hit the water knee deep, she dove head first, taking on the next wave. She came up out of the water giggling like a child on a hot summer day in a kiddie pool in the backyard under a water hose. I thought to myself, this girl is crazy! There's no telling what's in that water! It's dark, and it's cold! None of that mattered to her though - she felt alive. Jon Buchanan, another close friend and business partner, who was also with us, followed her into the water. So, I decided to join.

It wasn't until the following day that I realized why she was so excited about splashing around in cold salt water after dark. Tasha hadn't visited a beach in a couple of years and due to her ailments she couldn't be exposed to large amounts of sunlight. She couldn't even use sunscreen. I noticed her strict diet over the next few days as well. Every single thing, to the exact specifications, was meticulously planned out ahead of time. Alarms rang from her phone several times a day as a reminder to take this supplement or eat this food or drink that concoction.

Despite very low energy and very little sleep, she pushed through mental walls recruiting new customers and business partners. She mentored existing team members, hosted training calls and stood before other people (who were completely unaware of her war within) and delivered superb presentations. Up until that point, I knew who Tasha Eizinger was, but I didn't know what Tasha Eizinger was going through. That week I found out what Tasha Eizinger was made of.

The passion in her voice, the resiliency in her eyes, the confidence in her posture, the joy in her laugh, the resolve of her spirit and the size of her heart wouldn't let lost hope hang around much longer. Her strength to endure the pain and her willingness to do whatever it takes over a **two year period** inspired me and many others, to say the least. It was her decision to stay focused on what was possible, versus what was probable, that made all the difference. Faith in what was possible required daily servings of excitement. And her excitement was contagious!

Today, she is happier and healthier than she's ever been. What once felt like building her business from her "death couch" (because she couldn't even climb the stairs to the bedroom), turned into traveling the country, building her business now from wherever she chooses. Another one of her many dreams have come true. By standing up and digging in, when many people would've given up and given in, her and her husband Burke are now expecting their first little miracle. That's definitely something to be excited about! Oh, and she still has the popcorn maker that Jon and I bought her at Target in Glenwood Springs, when plain popcorn with rice bran oil and a pinch of sea salt was one of the few healthy snacks she could enjoy.

> *It is easy enough to be happy when life goes by like a song, but the person worthwhile is the person with a smile when everything goes dead wrong.*
> -Unknown

* * * * *

For me, excitement is the bridge from risk to action. Excitement is the belief that there are far better things ahead than any we leave behind. Believing that, I wake up each day excited to go out and meet my future and stake my claim. Excitement keeps me alive.

As I took shots to the chin, found myself in tight situations, grew frustrated that things weren't happening fast enough, I realized that those failures and adversities were developing me as a man. The maturation that took place conditioned me to view obstacles as opportunities. If you can stay positive and make that mental shift, then you can see your dream through.

Success doesn't belong to the person who is the most excited and wants it the most. Success belongs to the person who stays excited and wants it the longest. Some people never experience their dream or fulfill their destiny because they can't stay excited long enough. People who are unable to motivate themselves must be content with mediocrity, no matter how impressive their talents. But as for you, throw yourself into what you are pursuing. Whatever you are pursuing is also pursuing you. Go get it! Make it happen! Stay excited!

Excitement Notes

_____

_____

_____

_____

_____

_____

_____

_____

_____

_____

_____

_____

_____

_____

_____

D.R.E.A.M.

4

A is for ACTION

*The world is divided into people who do things
and people who talk about doing things. Belong
to the first group - there is far less competition.*

-John Mason

A month after my final day of teaching, I remember waking up one morning and asking myself: *What on earth do I do now?* I was so accustomed to a routine - a set schedule that told me when to wake up, what time to be at work, when I could eat lunch, how much time I could spend with my family and friends, and even when I could be sick. I never realized it before, but there was security in someone else telling you what to do and when to do it. They do all the thinking for you. You just have to show up. I was now responsible for it all. I took a huge risk and I was excited, and now it was time to manage that decision. You've heard this before: "where the rubber meets the road." Well, this was that place. It was time to get busy.

No Other Option

The honeymoon stage of leaving my job was over. It was official like a referee with a whistle - I was my own boss; the CEO of me. I set my own schedule. If it was going to be, it was up to me. Decisions determine our destiny. I had to decide to act. The only problem I had was... I didn't know

69

what to do. Just as a coffee mug reads that my little brother presented to me as a congratulatory gift:

RETIRED, WHAT THE #*@!! DO I DO NOW?

(As a side note, that's exactly what the mug reads. I typically don't sip coffee or tea from mugs that are stamped with choice words. That's not my style.)

I had just returned home from my first trip to Las Vegas with Luke Curry, a business partner and friend. Luke had already established himself as a strong young leader in our company and his results spoke volumes. Hungry to learn and eager to grow, I asked Luke several questions during that trip regarding his success in the business. He shared some of the good, the bad and the ugly that he'd experienced, but he also shared something that he claims put his business into motion. "I met a guy who was an icon in the industry and he mentored me on what could go right instead of what could go wrong."

Luke, similar to myself, decided to get off the sidelines of life, start playing to win and go after what he felt his family deserved. After the realization that "Corporate America" wasn't going to cut it, he made the decision to become an entrepreneur and go pro in network marketing. "I wanted to be a father, not just a provider," I've heard him say on many occasions.

With his first child only four months old, Luke sold his furniture to cover a few bills, started his business with a credit card (using OPM - Other People's Money) and he took massive action. The life he envisioned for his family kept him laser-focused and in 21 months they moved into a nearly 10,000 square foot home. It was a thank you gift to his wife for the some of the early sacrifices. And it was a pretty nice upgrade from the previous 600 square foot pad. Luke grew from a 24 year old gym manager, building someone else's dream, into a relentless entrepreneur who owned his time thanks to a decision to build his own empire.

Luke affirmed for me on that trip to Vegas that it was his reckless abandonment and relentless pursuit of his goals that produced his results. He told me that he woke up each day and said to himself in the mirror, "Everything about my family's livelihood depends on what I do today!" His reason *why* was strong enough. He sought out wise counsel and only took advice from the people who were where he wanted to be. He worked with a fourth quarter mentality - talking to people, talking to more people and talking to many more people.

That weekend, I learned a few valuable lessons, but mainly this: **greatness is in all of us, but most people are okay with being average.** One separator between average and great is action. While most people spend time getting ready to get ready, shuffling papers, jotting down notes and wishing upon a star, Luke puts feet to his dream. He acts. And by that, I don't mean he plays a role; I mean he goes to work.

Gettin' to It

Einstein said: "Nothing happens until something moves." After that Vegas rendezvous it settled in that no one was going to call me and ask me to build my business. I was no longer paid for my time; I was now paid for results and productivity. And the same bills that had to be paid when I had a job still had to be paid. What a travesty.

To put in perspective what happened next, we can point to a text message that I sent to a young man who I met by divine appointment one day just after wrapping up lunch with a friend from church. After we met, he reached out to me for support, asking specifically what I did to "overcome the loss of momentum."

My reply:

> ... Continue to develop myself, keep my goals & why in front of me, & invest my time in people who are positive, passionate, persistent, & patient. But above all else, continue taking consistent action every single day... because action is faith. I don't have any secrets - I just refuse to quit. Life will give you what you accept. It will also give you what you fight for.

After several trips to the beach to build the market that I previously mentioned, it completely folded. Someone told me that it's easier to give birth than it is to raise the dead. What that means is it's important to continue building a business looking for new people versus trying to drag others across the finish line. That same idea applies to other aspects of life. There were even some people who joined the team who went into witness protection the very next day - checking out quicker than they checked in. I've even had family members ask me to never contact them ever again.

I can recall a time when I couldn't afford a hotel room, so I slept in my car. On another occasion, in Atlanta, Robbie Davis (currently the second highest money earner in the US in my company) unselfishly saved the day. I swiped my card for a room and due to a late arrival of commissions on my card that afternoon, my card declined. It's almost as if when he stepped into the lobby of the downtown hotel that he had a "Jeremy Needs Some Help Radar" and he reached over my shoulder to give his card to the young man checking me and said with compassion and confidence, "I got it."

Calls stretching to different time zones required me to be awake at 2:00 and 3:00 AM. Many miles have been traveled on interstates when most people are fast asleep counting sheep. I've sat in living rooms in towns that I didn't know existed with people who were once complete strangers.

There have been many times when I've been distracted, failing to keep the main thing the main thing. One of those times I pulled into my driveway after a road trip to find a notice on the front door of my apartment that my water had been cut off. There have been times when tears welled up in my eyes as the collection plate drew closer during the offering on Sundays because I was so scared to let go of my tithe. I didn't trust that God could do more with 10 percent than I could do with 90 percent. What I'm saying is this: taking action hasn't always been sunshine, rainbows and yellow brick roads. I know what it feels like to "rob Peter to pay Paul" and even Pam to pay Paulette (there's a new one for you!). Close friends quit and I had to press on because they simply didn't have the vision I had or want what I wanted.

Through it all, I've continued to do what the late Jim Rohn, success coach and personal development trainer, teaches when he expounds on The Parable of the Sower from The Bible: kept on sowing the seed, kept on sharing the story, kept on making an invitation. Why? Because I knew from the beginning that I had an excellent seed and if I shared a good idea long enough, it would fall on good people. **My heart kept telling me to dream big, steadfastly believe and labor with love.** Chris Estes and Jason Keltner seemed so far away and still do at times. Through consistent action, though, I grew tougher and stronger. **Consistency of applied action inevitably leads to success, and it births resiliency in the process.** Resiliency, in return, builds a WHATEVER IT TAKES attitude.

The best and worst part of engaging in consistent action is the fact that it's pretty simple. Whatever you are pursuing can usually be broken down into a few fundamental productive activities. Simple means they are easy to do, but also easy not to do. Depending on how committed to your dream you are and how strong your why is, that will determine your outlook on the simple activities. I like to look at them as fundamentals, just like I did as a basketball player. Although becoming a great basketball player does require developing some skills, all of those revolve around a few basic things: dribbling, passing, shooting, and defending.

How often you work on the basic activities that are going to give you the most bang for your buck, day-in and day-out, that will determine your level of success. Knowing what to do helps to narrow the focus. And remember the old adage: hard work beats talent when talent fails to work hard.

The sad truth for most people is they have a dream, but they never wake up and go to work!

> *Most people know what they need to do, they just don't do it. It all comes down to discipline. I do it because I'm afraid of being average.*
> -Will Weaver

I Decided to Ask

Part of my action plan became tying myself to people who were better than me. With no one else in my home to answer to, I decided to ask for the time of people in my business and life who had what I wanted and were where I wanted to be. Nothing was tying me down from traveling to meet with these highly influential and successful people. I basically camped out with some of them, just ask Greg Bibb. When I met him and his wife, Tamara, at a leadership retreat, I followed him around with a pen and pad jotting down everything he said. When they tried to close it down for the evening one night that weekend, I knocked on their bedroom door. "Dude, we're trying to get some sleep," he responded. I wanted to know how a power couple did that, too!

Greg made a verbal contract with me that he would work closely with me to provide mentorship through my last few months of teaching. I dialed into his team calls for additional training. We had accountability and goal setting calls at the beginning of each week. He even shot me a text on Monday mornings, reminding me that it was the first day of the rest of my life and one of the last Mondays that I would be working for someone else. He helped me keep my eyes on the prize. He even invited me to his home. This was huge for me, because it gave me the opportunity to see what life was like for Greg. To my surprise, it was simple, just like mine.

> *Most of us begin by looking for worthy models to follow by reading about them in books. Start there. But don't leave it at that. Look for people who will give you access to their lives.*
> -John C. Maxwell

The best part about building my friendship with Greg and his family, and having his support, is that I've seen *him* grow tremendously in the process. In order to help someone else grow, you have to grow and keep growing. On the flipside, I've been harassed by all three of his pets. Kiki (one cat) pooped in the shower moments before I entered the bathroom to freshen up one morning. While leaning on the kitchen counter, Lizzie (the other cat) pounced on me, sinking all four sets of claws into my back as I was speaking on a live conference call. Braxton (the dog) tried to take my hand off in the theater room, during a movie, when I reached over for a friendly rub. I think it was their way of hazing me and welcoming me to the family.

While interviewing every other top earner that I could, not only did I immediately apply what they shared, but I also started to find some common denominators in what I was collecting. Some of the same ideas and principles were shared over and over again. Some things I implemented worked; some didn't. Some things I was good at; others I wasn't. Either way, I was able to learn the most important things that gave me the best shot at success, enabling me to stay active.

Here are the tools I gathered for my toolbelt that have helped build my philosophy:

1. Don't mistake activity for productivity.
2. A goal without a deadline is merely a wish.
3. Take care of your temple - exercise regularly.
4. Procrastination is a dream thief.
5. You become what you hang around.
6. Service to many leads to greatness.
7. It takes ten years to become an overnight success.
8. If you ask not, you have not.
9. Work harder on yourself than you do on your job/business.
10. Take good notes.
11. Everybody needs an accountability partner.
12. Wherever you are, be *all* there.
13. Success is not a place; it's a journey.
14. Find a mentor.
15. Do more than what you're paid to do.
16. Pray like it depends on God and work like it depends on you.

I could go on and on sharing the nuggets and pearls that I recorded. I learned how important it was to write things down. **Putting pen to pad and seeing your dreams on paper is critical in order to see your dreams come true.**

I learned that it was okay to be obsessed with my dream. Obsessed is a word the weak and lazy use for passionate. I learned how to dream big dreams - dreams so big that they scared me; so big that people would laugh at them. That translated for me: God-sized dreams. So, I started dreaming so big that the only way they could become a reality is if He intervened. Me and the "Big Guy" are working together now on a few things.

For me, the most powerful of the tools I picked up was: work harder on yourself than you do on your business. It held true that if you go to work on you, your business will go to work for you. Does this only apply to business? Of course not. It's the underlying theme that we are all in the *people business* and people do business with people they like. It you want to grow and accomplish a big dream, you have to become a more attractive person - a person of interest and value. Then, and only then, will you become necessary to the world. And if you become necessary to the world, the world will pay you your own price.

> *You can have more because you can become more.*
> -Jim Rohn

Another action tip from that list that served me well, and still does is: you become what you hang around. This doesn't just apply to people; it applies to your entire environment. This challenged me to get very intentional about selecting my associations. It's been said that we are the average of our five closest associations. So, now knowing I had to fuel my journey with the right people, books and CD's, I decided to surround myself with the best that I could find.

It's one thing to have a dream, but it's another ball game to manage the dream and protect it. In order to protect mine, I began limiting certain associations, expanding certain associations and completely terminating some associations. **I developed a philosophy that if someone in my life didn't want to see me grow, that someone had to go.**

Thus, a few good men (and women for that matter) were politely asked to exit the treehouse.

Dream Builders & Dream Stealers

When I decided to wake up and win, I started classifying the associations in my life into two categories: Dream Builders and Dream Stealers. I'm not going to necessarily say that everyone who doesn't want to help you, wants to harm you, but if you're like me, you want to keep the categorization simple. Heck, I get overwhelmed and confused when there's too many options to choose from in the grocery store. Whoever came up with the acronym KISS - "Keep It Simple Stupid" - certainly had me in mind.

A Dream Builder is someone who supports you, encourages you, breathes life into your mission, even circles your success in prayer. They celebrate your victories as if they were their own. You can pull from their strengths to complement your weaknesses. Some will be friends and some will be fans. Do your best to let them know how much you appreciate their role in your miracle process. **It will be those people, with whom over time, you look back and realize that the manifestation of a dream is, in large part, about the quality of relationships you create and the quantity of experiences you share.**

> *No one is useless in this world who lightens the burdens of another.*
> -Charles Dickens

A Dream Stealer is someone who can suck the life out of you. They may not always openly express it, but they doubt you. Your dream makes them question their vision and forces them to look in the mirror to assess their comfort zone. Even without knowing so, they're just negative - always *wishing* for the best, but expecting the worst. Some will be enemies, others will be skeptical bystanders. Love them all, anyway. Don't freak out if you start to notice a positive correlation between your growth and your number of haters. That's just the way it is. If that bothers you, then maybe greatness isn't for you.

> *If you are successful, you will win some unfaithful friends and some genuine enemies. Succeed anyway.*
> -Kent M. Keith (adopted by Mother Teresa)

Most problems I've encountered in life can be tied to a given relationship. Every single thing we do impacts someone else. Every relationship I have had and currently do have can be tied to my self-esteem and character. You typically attract that which you are, right? And who you are is tied to your heart. So, to tie this all together, if everything begins as a matter of the heart, then as you grow yourself you will begin to exercise those "dream receptors" and develop a form of discernment over who you build relationships with. In turn, you will actively recruit for the "home team," as I like to call it, or the group of people who classify as Dream Builders.

> *The asset I most value, aside from health, is interesting, diverse, and long-lasting friends.*
> -Warren Buffett

A Dream is a Verb

Wake up each day and take a step in the direction of your dreams. Just take action! It may not be a lot or as much as you would like to do on a given day, but a little bit is *something*.

Action will answer questions. Action will solve problems. Action will form winning habits. Doors open for those who decide to *do* versus those who just *exist*. Any achiever will tell you that there were days, even weeks, where it felt like they weren't covering much ground. It's in those moments that you learn to appreciate The Slight Edge Principle and The Compound Effect. Through consistency of applied action, whether it was sending an email on my lunch break in between classes or fielding a call on my way home from practice, I matured. I developed confidence. I began to appreciate the simplicity of daily disciplines as well as the mental toughness that it takes to stay focused.

Like me, through a series of small wins (and some won't feel like wins, trust me) you will find out that all you need to do is keep moving. Consider the African parable of the Lion and the Gazelle:

> *Every morning, in Africa, a Gazelle wakes up. It knows that it must run faster than the fastest Lion or it will be killed. Every morning, a Lion wakes up. It knows that it must outrun the slowest Gazelle or it will starve. It doesn't matter whether you are a Lion or a Gazelle: when the sun comes up, it's time to start running!*

We already know what would happen if the Lion or the Gazelle took a day off. But I have a question for you: are you okay with accepting the consequences of conceding on your life's purpose and your big dream? If you stop running, what happens to you? What will that mean for your family? What could that mean for people who are waiting to hear your story? My friend, Barry Daulton, a very successful tax professional and franchise business owner, shared a story with me about Paul Orberson, arguably the greatest networker of all time. He mentioned Paul's attempt to give up on his dream, but when he tried to look his daughter in the eye and tell her, he couldn't go through with it. He couldn't bare the thought of years passing and knowing that he didn't have the courage and the guts to win for his own children. His decision to press on, no matter what that looked like from day-to-day, resulted in a business that would break records for producing over $1,000,000 a month several months consecutively.

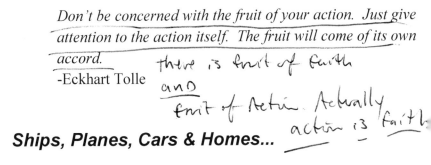

> *Don't be concerned with the fruit of your action. Just give attention to the action itself. The fruit will come of its own accord.*
> -Eckhart Tolle

there is fruit of faith and fruit of Action. Actually action is faith

Ships, Planes, Cars & Homes...

Most people don't know this, but one of the hardest things I have ever done was leave teaching. I had no idea that I was even making a difference. But when I informed my students that I wouldn't be returning for the second semester in my final year, and that I would be moving in a new direction, it was an emotional day in my classroom. On that day, I learned that the best part of the day for some kids was being at school. Some wanted to escape the realities of their home, and the best part of being at school, for some, was being in *my* classroom. That touched me more than I can tell you - it humbled me beyond measure. But it reassured me I was making the right decision, because I had a moral obligation to continue growing to show these kids what it looks like to passionately pursue what you want. The message I left with the kids that day was a call to action. I challenged them:

> *What are ships designed to do? They're built for sailing. What are planes put here for? They're made to fly. What about a car? What's a car here for? It's made to drive. And what about a home... what's it built for? Living. Finally, I ask you, what are you made to do? Here's what I think: You were engineered for accomplishment, built for greatness, designed for a perfect plan, crafted for a very important reason! You were made to go, do, love, work, and serve! You weren't placed here to merely exist!*

After those parting words, I had to walk the walk, or face the reality that I would be another male figure in the lives of many whose words meant nothing, because they weren't backed by activity.

* * * * *

Don't be the farmer who fails to plant the seed but is foolish enough to expect the crop to come in. **Some people never experience their dream or fulfill their destiny because they live in "Procrastination Nation" or on "Someday Isle."** Some people do take action, but they don't stay consistent and they end up nonexistent. If you dare to dream, are willing to take risks, stay excited, and commit to consistent action, success is just around the corner.

It won't happen overnight. Your prayers may not be answered immediately. But that's part of the set up. If achieving greatness were easy, don't you think everyone would have a plate full of it? You're going to screw up from time-to-time; that's also part of the set up. You can feel good about the fact that you probably won't mess anything up as bad as I have! I'll be the first to tell you: I haven't gotten it right even *half* the time! I may never get it right, but that hasn't stopped me from doing *something*. At the end of the day, talk is cheap and action speaks. State your claim, then go stake your claim. Go get it!

Action Notes

D.R.E.A.M.

5

M is for MOMENTUM

And as we let our own light shine, we unconsciously
give other people permission to do the same.
-Marianne Williamson

Our dreams want to see if we have what it takes to overcome the obstacles that will show up in our path. Our dreams want to see how we react to our mistakes and failures along the way. Our dreams want to see if we deserve them. If we pass the test, our success will serve as a path for others to prosper. This will serve as the foundation of a life of meaning and significance. That's what I call momentum. What I've come to find out on the roller coaster called dream in the theme park of life is this: the Dream Giver, as Bruce Wilkinson calls Him, wants to use me... if I persist, remain patient, and stay positive. In doing just that, I've experienced breakthroughs and impacted people in ways that I never thought possible. Some of those experiences have been a direct result of clearly defined, written goals, and some have come when I least expected, even temporarily disguised as failure or defeat.

Persistence, patience, positive provide momentum

Like Mike

72-10... That's the record of what stands as the best regular season in NBA history, posted by the Chicago Bulls in 1995-96. If we're just talking numbers, that would make them the best team in NBA history. I'm a little partial anyway, because I was born in 1984, the year Michael "Air" Jordan entered the league. He was one of my childhood heroes. The Bulls closed the '96 season with an NBA Championship, besting Seattle in the Finals, closing the year with an overall record of 87-13.

What's even more impressive, that single season was one of six that ended with an NBA Championship in the same decade for the Bulls: '91, '92, '93, '96, '97, '98. If there's an example of momentum, it's the 90's Bulls led by Phil Jackson.

The two year break between both three-peats had much, if not everything, to do with MJ's first retirement. It's a clear example of what the level of play - the expectation, the passion, the skill, the work ethic - that a single person can provide for the team around them. His influence extended much farther than the hardwood, though.

Michael Jordan may have single-handedly solidified the globalization of the professional athlete. When IMAX put him on the biggest screen in cinema in 2000 (*Michael Jordan to the Max*), the producers said it was because he was the only athlete on the planet who was larger than life. It's an ode to the stamp he left on the sports world. Every kid who grew up when I did, who had the dream to *be like Mike,* remembers the feeling that brewed up inside them as the Bulls starting lineup was announced on WGN. What kid didn't dunk a paper wad, with their tongue hanging out, through a wire clothes hanger on their closet door? And still today, what adult doesn't pause when they're flipping through channels on the tube and they see "His Airness."

The legacy that Mike has left is a direct result of *The D.R.E.A.M. Principle* at work. When a teacher told him he should join the Armed Forces or that he should pursue something math related, because that's where the money was, he **dared** to play basketball. After his father's tragic death and three rings under his belt, searching for new meaning in his life, he took a **risk** by leaving basketball to play baseball. During his path to basketball mastery, people were drawn to him because of his zeal, his charm, and his level of **excitement**. It took humble beginnings in the league, taking lessons from the Showtime Lakers, Detroit Bad Boys, and the original Boston Big Three, before he led the Bulls to an iconic run. But it was his **action** that proved he was not only the most talented in the gym every day, but he was the hardest worker in the gym every day. He used the bricks of failure to build steps so he could climb to greatness. And on his way to greatness, he carried others with him while inspiring millions. His **momentum** has been monumental. Ask anyone who has played the game of basketball since he blessed it with his presence.

Here is why Michael Jordan is a dreamer: *He got back up* to hit The Shot over Craig Ehlo in Cleveland, *after being knocked down* the previous night by missing three free throws that could have closed the series. The Cavs owned the Bulls during the regular season with six wins in six tries. Most people believe that the infamous right to left floater at the buzzer in the 1989 Playoffs was the mark of the beginning of the dynasty. What sealed his legacy (with what many would consider stole the rights to the title: "The Shot") was the crossover pull-up jumper over Bryon Russell of the Utah Jazz in game six of The Finals in 1998. His picture perfect follow through closed a second three-peat.

*If you're trying to achieve, there will be roadblocks. I've
had them; everybody has had them. But obstacles don't
have to stop you. If you run into a wall, don't turn around
and give up. Figure out how to climb it, go through it, or
work around it.*
-Michael Jordan

Gloria

I booked a several flights at the close of 2013 to various
locations to open 2014 with a bang. The first stop was the
Baltimore, D.C. area. Business was booming, our team had
just broken new ranks and set new records, and I had the
opportunity to gift Caroline (the Corolla) to my sister,
Jessica, for Christmas. (All the credit goes to a team full of
committed dreamers who decided to build something
beautiful on the lot they've been given in life.) Pulling up to
her house with the entire family and watching her open the
door, with Taylor by her side and Kayleigh on her hip (my
nieces), was a dream come true.

A couple of months prior, per the recommendation of a close
friend, I read Bruce Wilkinson's *The Prayer of Jabez* the
morning of my 29th birthday. Praying the same prayer that
Jabez prayed and millions pray today, I believe God
scheduled me for one of His divine appointments on a
connecting flight to the east coast. I sat next to a wonderful
soul, and her name was Gloria and she was headed to
Virginia.

It was a situation where I look back today and feel as if God
was waiting for me to stand up for Him, and He would then
reveal a secret to me. That book taught me that He favors

the bold, honors the faithful, and rewards the diligent. It also opened my spiritual eyes for opportunities to help others.

> *You can trust Him that He will never send someone to you whom you cannot help by His leading and strength. You'll nearly always feel fear when you begin to take new territory for Him, but you'll also experience the tremendous thrill of God carrying you along as you're doing it.*
> -Bruce Wilkinson

I could tell Gloria was overwhelmed by something, but I was tired and I'm a boss when it comes to napping on big birds. The Holy Spirit prodded me to strike up a conversation. After a heartfelt pow-wow that covered the whole gamut - faith, family, finances, fitness and fun - she shared that my enthusiasm for life and encouraging words helped her realize that she had stopped growing and dreaming. Little did I know I had something that could help a senior citizen blaze a new trail. C.S. Lewis once said: "You are never too old to set another goal or to dream a new dream." But here's where it gets good. Before we stepped off the plane, we prayed together. And after that prayer, she softly put her hand over mine to gather my full attention - it was a touch that expressed: *I am with you.* She looked me in the eye and said, "Son, you could write a best-seller. Wherever you are going and in whatever you do, don't waste time - you know how busy the devil is! It's a pleasure, so nice to know a young multimillionaire. I pray that you will be the biggest tither at your church…"

Here's where it gets even better. At that time, I had considered a slim possibility in the future of writing a book, but I honestly didn't think I was qualified - I didn't think I had

*If farms the bold
hours the truthful
rewards the diligent*

accomplished anything that gave me permission to do such a thing. I didn't have the Les Brown story that I heard him share, live, that fall in Salt Lake City. I had a dream to encourage people all over the world, but I had no idea how that would happen. As we eluded to earlier, when we decide to get busy about our work, the how is none of our business, we just have to have enough faith to act and the conviction to see it through. So here's what I did: continued to build my business and pray, every, single day, The Jabez Prayer. Here's what I found out: whatever you are seeking it is also seeking you.

> *And Jabez called on the God of Israel saying, "Oh, that You would bless me indeed, and enlarge my territory, that Your hand would be with me, and that You would keep me from evil, that I may not cause pain!" So God granted him what he requested.* -1 Chronicles 4:10 (NKJV)

If You Don't Quit, Things Start Happening

Do you remember the daunting task of pushing the merry-go-round when all of your friends jumped on first and started barking orders? Do you remember how hard it was to take the first couple of steps? I bet you also remember that feeling when you started to gain some momentum - your friends started cheering. Once that big thing got to rolling wide open, you could step back and just throw a hand in every couple of rotations with a love tap to keep it going. If you were like me, you couldn't wait to get it going because you loved the thrill of jumping on while it was moving! I'm sure there were even times you reached out to slow it down (thanks to that one kid who cried out that it was going too fast). Do you remember that jerk you felt when you grabbed a bar? The human saucer dish may have even pulled you with it. That's because momentum is a force to reckon with. But, it takes time to build. *momentum takes time to build*

In network marketing, momentum is a phenomena that sends a business center into another orbit. Simple activities that have been practiced and duplicated in an organization begin to compound exponentially. Sometimes, the growth of a team can grow in spite of you - with or without your efforts. It's a special situation. People start joining your team due to sheer excitement. Your determination proves that work is worth it and your action proves that you deserve it. With the right company, it can mean tens of thousands of lives positively impacted in your community, state, country, or even across the world!

We can also look at the marathoner who pounds the pavement for 26.2 miles. This is a prime example of the idea that many people *start* the race, but very few *finish*. What's the difference between those who do finish and those who don't? Patience, positivity and persistence. I've heard stories of runners hitting a "brick wall" at a particular mile marker. Everything in their body is screaming no and wants to shut down. The champion who has a strong enough reason why, remembers the hundreds of miles invested in training and the activities that took a back seat to this pursuit... they push through that wall. And when they push through that wall, it's almost like a coast to the finish line. How one could "coast" for the last five to eight miles is a mystery to me. I really don't have the desire to find out, so we'll lean on the testimonies of the experts. But you get my point. It's called momentum.

The same thing happens in a basketball game, or maybe any other sporting event; especially team sports. When a team is on a run, you have players making plays, getting stops and knocking down shots that they probably wouldn't make, get or hit. Confidence grows, excitement builds and decisions become totally instinctive. You start operating out of expectancy rather than fear and hesitancy. Are you still making mistakes? Of course. But are you focused on them? No. It's as if mentally you have developed a bad case of amnesia and ripped the rear view mirror off. No looking back. I can remember the basket even feeling like it was three times its original size, like the difference between the front windshield and the back glass in a car. During a brief stint my senior year of high school, my team led our entire state in three point field goal percentage. Most people would consider that the best shooting team, in that case. With that momentum, I averaged over 25 points a game in a holiday tournament and I shot over 60 percent from the arch for nearly a third of the season. I can recall taking shots and turning around to head back to the other end of the floor, because it felt like it was money (slang hoops terminology for a made basket) when it left my hand.

In all of these examples, someone had to start *somewhere*. The merry-go-round had to have that first push, the network marketing team had to have that leader who took action, the marathoner had to lace up the shoes and brave the elements early in the morning or late at night, and the basketball team had to start conditioning on opening day, several weeks before the regular season began. With consistency, things happened, because someone didn't quit. For me, things began to happen as I traveled down this road less traveled. My story about Gloria is an example. Another includes a bucket list weekend in Orlando.

Mobile Office

Jon Buchanan was looking for a way out of his current situation. He was "time bankrupt," as he likes to say. Thanks to a particular philosophy on money along with good old-fashioned hard work, he took on responsibilities at an early age that most people wouldn't dare touch. While in college, he not only ran track and cross-country at the same school I attended, he also managed two businesses (carpet cleaning and medical supplies), and continued working on the family farm, helping raise approximately 300 head of beef cattle. Friend, that's called busy!

> *To me, it's a risk to not own a business. Working for someone else is like slavery to me… I knew that at any time I could go get a job if I had to.*
> -Jon Buchanan

After his introduction to a home based business opportunity, Jon ran with it. And after ten months of building that business along with the 80-plus hour work weeks he was already putting in; some weeks 100, he sold his two other companies for one reason: stress. Jon had zero time for what was at the top of his priority totem pole. By helping people help people, he's now a six-figure earner in the industry.

Although Jon and I grew up just a few miles apart and attended the same college, we never ran around with the same crowd. So, it wasn't until our paths crossed at a leadership retreat that we began holding each other accountable, mostly from a business and fitness standpoint. Now, we have traveled thousands of miles together, presented in living rooms all across the country and have had each other's back through the good, the bad and the ugly of growing as a young men in a world that invites and encourages you to back down at every corner.

Something happens, though, when you don't quit. We had an "A-ha!" moment in Orlando one Monday morning in May. After connecting with some incredible people while growing our business, Jon and I were invited down to Bay Hill for the annual Arnold Palmer Invitational where Tiger Woods would be defending his 2012 win. To say that I was excited is an understatement. I had literally written on my "2013 Bucket List" at the beginning of the year: *See El Tigre play LIVE!* The crazy thing is, I made zero plans to actually make that happen.

When I left teaching, it piqued the interest of a guy named Brad. I worked with his wife Jennifer. After Brad partnered with me, he extended the invitation to join our team to his sister, Jamie, who at the time was working at a golf academy in Orlando. She noticed that I enjoyed golf after peeping some activity I shared via social media (we actually call that "creeping").

It was my first PGA event and the atmosphere was incredible. Seriously, the weather literally couldn't have been any better... spring, Orlando, golf, and ice cold Strawberry Arnold Palmers. Watching one of the world's greatest golfers walk out onto the number one tee was super cool. Overly excited, I nearly fell victim to cell phone confiscation due to the tournament policy that I was unaware of.

Since the weather couldn't get any better, it decided to get about as bad as it could. During Sunday's final round a storm came through, bringing Category 1 hurricane winds. Most people, like myself, downplayed the possible severity and assumed that it would be something that passed quickly. Play was suspended, my meager umbrella failed, trees were snapping, rain was falling like it was pouring from a bucket (I nearly tapped into my inner-Noah) and a transformer went boom, right next to the course due to a streak of lightning. The sky above the treeline lit up with an orange-red hue. I thought to myself: *Holy smokes, I've read about this in Revelations! God, if it's my time to go, what a way to check out?!*

It was announced that all tickets from the final round would be honored the following day when play resumed. That morning when the horn sounded and Tiger teed off on the third hole, it hit me. There was no crowd. Where was everyone at? It was Monday... and they had to go back to work. Because of risk I had taken two years prior and simple activities that we had engaged in consistently, when I woke up that morning, I had earned more money for that week than I had ever earned in my best week teaching and coaching for 50-60 hours.

It was in that moment that I looked at Jon, grinning so big that I could eat a banana sideways and said: "So this is what it feels like? This is what young and free means!" Bay Hill was our mobile office, we were the CEO of our global enterprises and residual income was working in our favor. Owning my time became a little bit more tangible, so to speak.

The Bottom Line

Momentum is the discovery of a part of you that you didn't know existed. When you discover that part of you, and you begin to develop it, you reach a new level of awareness. You begin operating under a mindset that you can manifest anything that you choose to manifest in your life, if you focus your attention to it and you move toward it.

Momentum is the harvest of the seed that you planted and cultivated day-in and day-out. It's like the Chinese Bamboo Tree. It's planted and every single day for five years it is watered and it appears that nothing is happening. Let me repeat that: every single day for five years it is watered and it appears that nothing is happening. If this process is cut short, the tree will die in the ground. But after five years, the tree breaks the surface, and shoots to towering heights greater than 90 feet in less than six weeks. It's the reminder from Galatians (6:9) that we should "not grow weary of doing good, for in due season we will reap, if we do not give up."

Momentum is the favor that you experience after you brave the elements of the cold winters and dark nights of your dream. People, places, things, and ideas will conspire to serve your purpose and help you manifest your destiny. It will seem as if these resources will have called a meeting to huddle up and delegate who will come find you first. And they *will* come find you. It's the reciprocity of you waking up every single day and asking, "How may I serve? And who may I serve?"

Momentum is a place where life becomes an adventure. Great things are allowed to happen to you and for you because you have given yourself permission to enjoy the process. You have given yourself permission to fail. You have given yourself permission to be bad. You no longer view circumstances as good or bad, but rather as miracles or learning experiences.

Momentum is the opportunity that you give life to express itself through you. It brings with it great responsibility. You become a channel of energy. People are *drawn to* you. People are *inspired by* you. People *appreciate* you. Your mission becomes a beacon of hope for others. Your words and your actions are a lamp to others' feet. **People will no longer come to you and ask *why* you *do it*, but *how* you *did it*.** And because of you, others will be able to say, "I can, too!"

Momentum is the beginning of a life of meaning and significance. It's who you are becoming while on your way. It's also what my good friend, Clifton always says, "Do the right thing at the right time with the right motivation... Then, you will get the right results and more importantly, you will earn the right to expect others to do the same."

Momentum is also the realization that you will never "arrive." It's understanding that there is a responsibility that you have in the miracle process of life and that responsibility is to continue growing and stretching... doing and serving... loving and leading... hoping and helping. **It's your responsibility to leave this place better than you found it when you arrived here.** It's the understanding that what matters most on your tombstone is the dash between the years.

* * * * *

If you could earn more, shouldn't you? If you could become healthier, shouldn't you? If you could do better, shouldn't you? If you could learn more, shouldn't you? If you could become happier, shouldn't you? If you could have more fun, shouldn't you? Of course you should. But it is a process, just like writing this book was a process. I thought about giving up just as you have considered walking away from your dream, but I didn't and here we are with a message to share.

The achievement of a big dream is reserved only for the brave and the bold. Dreams don't become a reality overnight and prayers don't get answered immediately. That's not the setup here. If you don't like it, get your own planet and organize your own deal. But until then there are some rules to the game, and if you understand the rules, you can play to win instead of playing to not get beat.

If you don't quit, things simply start happening. You can't explain a lot of it; you just roll with it. And whatever goodness you have going for you at that point, be grateful for it, and share it with people. Give it away freely. The world is waiting for you to gain momentum and take flight. Go ahead, launch your dream!

Momentum Notes

_____

_____

_____

_____

_____

_____

_____

_____

_____

_____

_____

_____

_____

_____

_____

D.R.E.A.M.

6

Dreams Do Come True

This world is owned by people who have crossed bridges in their imagination before anyone else has.
-John C. Maxwell

Would you give me the opportunity to climb down inside of your head for just a moment. While I'm there, would you unlock the door to your heart? I want all access with your undivided attention. I want to close this book by helping you re-program your mind and rewrite your agreement with reality. Albert Einstein once said, "Imagination is everything. It is the preview of life's coming attractions." So let's begin this final chapter by stepping into our imagination. What I want you to do right now is visit jeremyandyou.com, select the Media tab, and hit the "Dreams Do Come True" video. Seriously - do it right now.

How did that make you feel? Does is it inspire you to know where your imagination can take you? Or are you let down because you can't see yourself as you already are what you would like to become? Did a slug fest between your regrets and your dreams surface? Who won? Were you envisioning a future of lost hope? Or did you picture a life well lived?

I don't know about you, but I don't want to get to the finish line of my life and find that all I did was exist. I want there to be depth and meaning attached to my name. I want the dash on my tombstone to count for something. I want people to say, "There was a guy who lived and died empty." And that's exactly what went through my mind while sitting in a room full of thousands of *high hopers* at the Salt Palace in downtown Salt Lake City in the fall of 2013. Les Brown, master motivator, was narrating his life along with sharing success principles, from the stage. It was as if he was spitting flaming darts of hope, enthusiasm and inspiration into the crowd. One of those darts pierced my heart. I'm not sure if the folks sitting next to me noticed, but I closed my eyes. His voice rang out as he claimed with confidence that whatever you seek to accomplish and desire to do, "IT'S POSSIBLE!" Tears escaped my clamped eyelids and ran down my cheeks when he shouted out, "Ladies and Gentlemen, not only is it possible, but IT IS NECESSARY!" I pictured an empty convention center, with the exception of two people: Les... and me. He looked at me and his final words were: "YOU HAVE GREATNESS IN YOU!," was like a gust of air that rushed into my lungs. It gave me life.

I opened my eyes, refocused to the stage, and knew in that moment that I was made for more than I was producing, because I am cut from the same cloth as Les Brown. And so are you.

> *Truly, truly, I say to you, whoever believes in me will also do the works that I do; and greater works than these will he do, because I go to the Father.* -John 14:12 (ESV)

What If...

What if you woke up tomorrow and went to work not just to pay the bills, but to make a difference. What if you decided right now to start doing something that gives your life meaning. I can't guarantee the outcome, because that is determined by what you choose to do or choose not to do, and that's not of my making. I can guarantee two things, however: (1) if you keep using "what if" to your disadvantage, you'll keep getting regrets; (2) if you start using "what if" in your favor, you'll start collecting dreams.

What if you wrote the song…
What if you took the class…
What if you moved to the city…
What if you joined the church…
What if you proposed to the girl…
What if you made the call…
What if you applied for the job..
What if you went on the mission trip…
What if you started the business…
What if you read the book…
What if you adopted the child…
What if you made the apology…
What if you tried out for the play…
What if you believed in yourself…
What if you traveled the world…
What if you got uncomfortable…
What if you did something you've never done before…
What if you surprise yourself with what you could accomplish…
What if you had childlike faith…
What if you trusted your heart…
What if you became a multi-millionaire…
What if it *did* work…
What if you asked for help…
What if your wildest dreams *did* come true…

What if you changed someone's life…

We all hold the same capacity to consider what our lives would look like on the upside of that common question. This one small tweak could be the change that sends your life to a new level.

Dreams do come true for people who think crazy things and say crazy sayings. Dreams do come true for the unrealistic and unreasonable. Dreams do come true for the misfits who challenge the norm. Dreams do come true for the select few who are able to see themselves as they already are what they would like to become. Dreams do come true for the weirdos who pray in the shower, then jump out to write something down so they don't forget it. **Dreams do come true for the people who are brave enough to actually try to change the world.**

Amanda, J.J. & Lauren

If you want to know if dreams do come true for people just like you, we can refer to Amanda, J.J. and Lauren.

The Thursday evening before my final week of teaching, my brother, Michael, and I slid down to Nashville for a celebratory meal at my favorite restaurant, B.B. King's. I got the usual: cajun carbonara. We raised our glasses to new beginnings and discussed the future. Our server - then a stranger, now a dear friend - Amanda Mackintosh was one of the gazillion dreamers who packed her bags and moved to "Music City" to sing the song on her heart. She worked her way through Belmont University, serving at local dives, to pay for studio time. She wrote songs from her downtown apartment with the company of her bestie, Mu-Shu, her pet pig (I even have a selfie with Mu-Shu). She sang her heart out because she believed her dream was possible. Then she met a girl just like her, named Carly, with a similar vision. The by-product of that serendipitous meeting is a tag-team now known as Aberdeen Green and their first album is called *The Oak Tree*.

> *At four years old I would tug on peoples' pant legs and ask*
> *if they wanted to hear me sing.*
> -Amanda Mackintosh

Less than a decade ago, NFL defensive end J.J. Watt, who now serves quarterback sacks, was serving large two toppings. He failed to report back to school after his first year at Central Michigan. So, he got a job and enrolled in a couple of classes at a local school. During a delivery, a young boy recognized Watt as a standout high school player in the area and questioned what he was doing working at Pizza Hut instead of playing football. After that wake-up call, he divorced his mediocre existence, went to work on himself and walked on at the University of Wisconsin-Madison. Three years later, he was selected as the 11th overall pick in the NFL Draft by the Houston Texans. From pizza to prosperity. His mantra today is: "Dream Big, Work Hard."

> *There were plenty of reasons why I shouldn't be able to*
> *make it and people reminded me often. But I had a dream*
> *and turned it into a goal.*
> -J.J. Watt

Lauren Hill scored the first two points of the 2014-15 NCAA basketball season. After being diagnosed with an inoperable brain cancer and only a short time expected to live, schedules were changed - games were moved up on the calendar. Why? Because when dreams are big and people are inspired, prayers are prayed, strings are pulled and big things happen. Mount St. Joseph had to move their home opener, which usually pulls about 100 fans, to Xavier University, because over 10,000 people wanted to be a witness and support the cause. Her courage to play and raise awareness for DIPG (Diffuse Intrinsic Pontine Glioma), inspired basketball icons such as LeBron James and Skylar Diggins and coaching legend Pat Summitt. Hundreds of thousands of dollars have now been raised for research all because Lauren had a dream of playing college basketball - something she once thought would never be possible due to her debilitating disease. If you want to the see her dream, live and in color, go to any social media forum and enter #Layup4Lauren in the search bar.

> *I wanted to wear that jersey and feel like a superhero, again.*
> -Lauren Hill

Do What You Love

When I began speaking on a small scale, introducing people to my business and sharing the story of the company, I noticed something. One evening, from the front of my living room, as I welcomed a couple of people to my humble abode, I clenched my fists and they felt cold and sweaty. This may sound somewhat silly to you, but it was a sign that what I was doing was the right thing. It was the same feeling I had before nearly every basketball game I had ever played while growing up. It was the result of a combination of several emotions - nervous, anxious, excited, scared and anything else you can think of that makes up that "I'm ready to rock/I'm ill equipped and unprepared" feeling.

As a reminder: "If you're doing what you love, you'll never work a day in your life." Les Brown says, "My definition of success is doing what you love to do and finding someone to pay you to do it." What about that? If you can do what you love and get paid for it, that's a pretty good deal!

I like to put it this way... **If you're not doing what you love and loving what you do, then you have two options: you can either change how you feel about what you do, or you can change what you do.** I think it's pretty simple. In a world where technology and information and "good opinions" from other people have the tendency to drown out our inner voice, I believe if you get still and listen, you can find what it is that you want to do.

It begins with what you enjoy. What are you good at? What do you love? What gives you energy? What gives you a sense of accomplishment? What would you do for free? Look to your heart. That's where your journey begins. Or if you have wandered off the trail leading to your dream, look to your heart. That's how you make your way back. **I believe that finding your calling is more important than finding your career.** And I believe you find your calling by listening to your heart. That's where your dream lies.

> *Do what you love; you'll be better at it. It sounds pretty simple, but you'd be surprised how many people don't get this one right away.*
> -LL Cool J

Pick Your Partners

I've referenced already the importance of the right associations. So, I'll try to bring this point home without being redundant. But the fact that it's been mentioned already should be a clue. When a teacher puts a heavy emphasis on something - repeats what he or she says... When something is bold, highlighted, underlined, or there's an asterisk by it... Yeah, that's what I'm getting at here. It's important. Do not miss this! **The people you associate with can and will make you or break you.**

Treat your dream like a massive global project, because it is. Thanks to zero degrees of separation in today's world, what you do or choose *not* to do, can impact someone on the opposite end of the planet. So, treat your associations like your own personal board of directors. If those select people are going to be the people that you spend the most time with, work closely with, trust your dream with and go to battle with, shouldn't you be choosy with who qualifies? A coach once asked me if I was going to war and I could take one person, who would I take in a foxhole with me. A friend once told me that you know who's got your back when it's moving day and it's raining outside.

Place some criteria around what you will or won't accept in your life when it comes to the people you hang around. They should be people who support you and also people who complement your weaknesses with their strengths. **If you think you can be a one man show, your dream will never grow.** And make sure you check their attitude at the door. When you hang out with winners, you get ideas and build dreams. When you hang out with losers, you make

excuses and get regrets. Separate yourself from the flakes.
Work with the willing and love the rest.

> *There is a destiny which makes us brothers; none goes his*
> *way alone. All that we send into the lives of others comes*
> *back into our own.*
> -Edwin Markham

Develop Yourself

If you want your dream to come true, a prerequisite is
learning how to develop yourself. People stop dreaming
because they stop learning. The phrase that you can't teach
an old dog new tricks chaps my rear end. It's one of those
sayings that sets me on fire, like when you ask someone
how they're doing and they reply, "You know, gettin' by..." or
"Workin' - stayin' busy..." or "Another day, another dollar" or
"I'm here..."

That nonsense drives me crazy. Part of what makes a
dream a dream, is that it's something that encourages you to
aspire to be more. It's something that forces you to grow in
order to manifest it. I like how Mark Batterson covers it:
"Your dream and destiny isn't just revealed in your natural
gifts and abilities; it is also revealed in the compensatory
skills you had to develop because of the disadvantages you
had to overcome."

It's sad the number of people who never pick up a book after
high school. But I'm right there with them. I was the dude
who hated to read. I certainly didn't think I would write a
book for someone else to read! The only book I read in high
school was *Of Mice and Men* (Steinbeck, 1993). I didn't
know that leaders were readers and learners were earners

You will learn from experience. That's life. And you will learn from wisdom. That's life lived by others. **But if you want to expedite the process of accomplishing your goals and living out your dream, give yourself a head start and an edge by developing yourself.** Read the autobiographies of people who have overcome insurmountable odds to do something great. Listen to positive and inspirational audio in your car or during your workouts. Exercise your mental muscle. Prepare yourself for success. Get ready for your date with destiny.

> *You will be the same person in five years as you are today except for the people you meet and the books you read.*
> -Charles Jones

Knee Pads

One of my closing thoughts, and I share this unapologetically, and it may sound somewhat scrambled, but I don't know how else *to* share it. So, here is this: **if you truly want to find your dream and fulfill your destiny, get in the presence of God.** Truth be told (don't let that freak you out; I've been telling the truth the whole time - scouts honor), I was scared out of my mind to do anything different than I have ever done. Feel free to call me "soft" if you want. But as I began moving toward my dream, I had doubts, just like you. I had worries, just like you. I had issues, just like you. And I still do. What I found out was: moving toward my dream was actually me moving toward God. I believe it's His divine design that you have a dream. So, when you move toward Him, He honors that and will begin opening doors and moving resources with His supernatural favor in attempt to anoint you. He wants to bless your effort to serve

His kingdom. But please don't take this out of context. God is not some genie in a bottle or a celestial Santa Claus in the sky. Your wish is not His command and His job is not to gift you every present on your Christmas list in order to fulfill your dream. His delight is in giving you what you *need* and watching you grow.

As I've grown from a male to a man, I have grown to appreciate Romans 8:28 more and more...

> *And we know that for all those who love God all things work together for good, for those who are called according to His purpose.*

Every morning, I get a reminder from my little blue accountability partner, my watch, at 8:28 a.m. that God can and will remove (what I think is) the good from my life to make room for the BEST. It's a reminder that as my Heavenly Father, He knows me better than I know me and He knows what's BEST for me. He knows you better than you know you; He created you. I need this reminder because I have the tendency (like you, maybe) to consider the removal of certain things in my life as a punishment for my sin. There is discipline, but discipline is different from pruning. As you pursue your dream, God wants to help you burn off your impurities to get down to the precious metal. And that metal, you and your gifts, are what you gift to the world.

I thought, what right do I have to build a business and write a book? **God responded, "*With Me*, what right do you NOT have?"** If there is one message that you take with you from this book and one message only, let it be this: **I am just as imperfect and broken as you.** But the grace and provision

of God takes nobodies and turns them into somebodies.
The stories of the crooks, thieves, liars, murderers and
betrayers that He took and turned into Warriors, Disciples
and Kings should give you hope. When the world tells you
that your dream is impossible, God will remind you that with
Him *nothing is impossible.* When your past comes looking
for you to tell you that it's time to come back, God will remind
you that you have a new home.

God never consults your past to determine your future.
-Mike Murdock

When I found out that I was much better off with Him than I
was without Him, things changed for me. My dreams got
bigger, my vision became clearer, my faith grew stronger.
It's evident that it hasn't been about the business, nor this
book. It's been about the man that I have become in the
process. The man that I have become in the process and
the person that you can and will become on your journey is a
person who learns how to submit their plans to the lordship
of Jesus Christ. God is the Master Editor, if you will, of your
story, your book, your movie. **If you lay it down, He will lift
it up. If you give it up, He will fill it up.** And when He has
approved your dream, you then have dominion over the
earth, under His will, to go out and build it. And when I say
build, I mean build it BIG!

One of my faith mentors, Michael Edwards, told me:
"There's something special that happens that one can't
explain when a man falls to his knees and asks for God's
help." Wayne Dyer told me from the speakers of my car that
"If prayer is you talking to God, then intuition is God talking
to you." So, I started scheduling daily appointments with
God. I started hitting my knees. I have a goal to pray so

much that I would need to pick up a pair of knee pads. I still don't even know if I'm praying for the right things. I'm learning. I'm learning that the more I pray, the more I can expect. I'm learning that **His ways are higher than my ways** and **His plans are better than my plans.** I'm learning that He can give you wisdom and truth that no person on the planet can provide. Since you are made in His image and since He grants us the gift of the Holy Spirit, thanks to the life that Jesus gave on the cross at Calvary, then what is on your heart is what you can and should pursue! That's your dream. *Go Buy!*

From my personal prayer journal:

God,

I am Yours. Where do You want me to go? Where can I represent You? Where is Your will? Tug at my heart. I AM WILLING and I AM WAITING. Let's GO!

Love,

Jeremy

I believe God would have been proud of me for producing my best work possible, but I felt like He wanted me to lay more of my heart on the line and show *you* that it's okay to be vulnerable. If I'm scrutinized for it, that's okay. I have a Protector. I'm not a human having a spiritual experience; I'm a spirit having a human experience. And what dreams I pursue aren't to please them; it's to please Him. It's His plan for us to serve His kingdom, shepherd His flock and steward His resources. How do we do that? Love Him and love people.

Everything changes when you come to know how valuable you are to God. He's *your* Heavenly Father. Your picture is on his refrigerator. **He will remind you that dreams do come true for people just like you, not because of what you can do, but because of what's already been done for you.**

> *I believe it honors God when we enjoy life and live it well. That means taking risks - sometimes failing, sometimes succeeding, but always learning. When you enjoy your life the lines between work and play begin to blur. We do what we love and love what we do. Everything becomes a learning experience.*
> -John C. Maxwell

Knock One Down for the Road

My dad used to tell me every time we wrapped up a hoop session: "Knock one down for the road, Jerm." What he meant was: never close it down and head to the house on a miss. So, here's my attempt to close down our time together on a make.

There is a fire that burns deep in the pit of my stomach for you and what you're capable of. It's my dream that you find your passion and your purpose. It's my dream that if you've lost hope, this book will urge you to get up and look for it. It's my dream that if you've been in a funk, you'll wake up and go to work. It's my dream that if you already know what you're put here to do, that you would set sail and go for it courageously and confidently.

Ask yourself this question: *If I died today, what dreams would die with me?* There's some good out in the universe that has your name on it. There is opportunity and abundance waiting for you. Only you can claim it. So, don't miss it! No greater agony exists on Earth than bearing an untold story inside of you. **Step into your greatness and refuse to die with your music still in you.** Refuse to arrive at your grave with your great mission unfulfilled. It's the difference between your dream being a burden or a blessing. Disregard the common consciousness and live up to your true potential. Your time is now! If you believe you're a winner, it's time to act like a winner!

On your way, some people will check out. You will see other people concede on their dream. I say to you: BE DIFFERENT. Ball out! **Declare that this will be the day that you toss the old script in the trash and rewrite your agreement with reality.** You are the Head Coach, the CEO, the General, the Director of your dream. No one else is going to come by and build it for you. But others will stop by when the time is right and build it *with* you.

Will it be hard at times? Yes it will! But will it be worth it? Absolutely! It won't be sunshine, rainbows, and yellow brick roads. It's not easy, but it is necessary. After all, what in life is worth anything that comes easy? What lessons do you learn? What strength do you gain? What blessing do you receive? If we got everything we wanted at the exact moment that we wanted it, this world might be an even more screwed up place. That's why your dream will require patience, positivity and perseverance. There will be disappointment. There will be failure. There will be pain. There will be moments when you doubt yourself. You will

[handwritten in right margin:] thing But I must get out of debt so the debt won't stop me from living life abundantly to live life abundantly But it's really because the want to

[handwritten at bottom:] It's not easy but it's necessary. I know this because he translated the spiritual necessity of doing it into my physical world's necessity of doing. I must because it needs doing on many levels, I thought it was because I was in Debt

ask, "God, why is this happening to me?" But whatever happens, do not give up on your dream.

More than likely you're not where you want to be. I hope that's the case. Not because I don't want what's best for you, but because I want you to be the person who never arrives and never stops growing. If you're in a place that you're not happy with, that's okay. Today is a new day. God has you right where He wants you, but He doesn't plan on keeping you there. You are important. You are a child of the King. Get excited about that! If you can't get excited, you're more than welcome to call me. I mean that - call me! I have plenty of excitement you can borrow! Probably enough for you, your mom, your Uncle Joe, and your baby sister's third cousin too! Can you tell that I'm excited about your future? It's because I believe in you!

You matter! You can make a difference! It's your right and responsibility! Take time to write down your dream and why you want to fulfill it, then go live it!

> *Everyday, millions of people have dreams. Don't ignore yours. Your dream may be your gift to the world. Pursue it; share it; live it.*
> -Clifton Lambreth

* * * * *

You may feel that with being a "published author" there's some higher level of credibility that comes with it. I don't think so. When I dared to dream, I didn't know anything about anything. When I decided to take a great risk, I hadn't learned much about much. But I did stay excited. I have learned that consistency of applied action is key. And I have now seen that momentum is things moving in you, through you and because of you.

All I decided to do was draw a line in the sand, be bold, break the mold, live out loud and stand out from the crowd. It's time for you to **DECIDE** too!

How do I know that dreams do come true? I know because this book is in your hands. It made its way from an iPhone 3GS, to a worn composition notebook that sits in a chair in the bedroom of a small duplex apartment, to a red Moleskin journal that's traveled the country, to the back corner of coffee shop after coffee shop. Paragraphs were formed from park benches all across the Commonwealth of Kentucky. It's the result of tiresome days and sleepless nights. Ideas were birthed in the middle of the highway during road trips, and notes were collected while the steering wheel was manned by a right knee. Ideas were scribbled on wet post-it notes, thanks to a light bulb that went off while in the shower. Ideas surfaced in airports from conversations with complete strangers. I even bought a Chromebook that wasn't in my budget in order to type it, because my old jalopy crashed. Stories were shared by several and wise counsel was given by many. It took time away from family and friends. Things I *wanted* to do took a backseat to the things I *needed* to do. It was double and triple circled in prayer. And here we are.

It's been a blessing to meet you here. I wish I could sit down with you, spend time with you, hear your story, and encourage you on your journey. I mean that. I am thankful that our dreams crossed paths. So, this now becomes a story not just about me. It's now a story about we - me and you... and it is to be continued.

Epilogue - Let's Do Lunch

You can have everything in life you want, if you will just help enough other people get what they want.
-Zig Ziglar

It was already 12:29 (half past noon, as some folks from my parts would call it), so I shot him a quick text: Am I at the correct one; just off of Old Hickory?! I was anxious, to say the least, but also a tad bit worried that I may be at the wrong O'Charley's. You wouldn't want to be late and disrespect the time of someone who is worth millions, right? When he confirmed that I was at the *only* O'Charley's in Brentwood, I politely asked the hostess to show me to my seat. She could've easily assumed that I was stood up for a lunch date due to my super early arrival. I had been waiting since 12:03. If you know me, being that early for an appointment is rare. My mom once said that my dad would be "late for his own funeral." Call me crazy, but I happened to think that was a pretty good idea. So, I followed his footsteps.

> *"How many total will be dining?,"* the young hostess asked.
> *"Two, please,"* I answered, questioning my simple math.
> *"Right this way,"* she replied.

En route to my seat, I glanced at my phone and noticed a Facebook text alert. It read: Celebrate with Clifton Lambreth today... I did everything but freak out - in the most nonchalant way possible, of course! In a society where people check their Facebook account at least 57 times per day, and social media not being the most important thing in the world, but ranking right up there next to oxygen, how could I have possibly overlooked the fact that today was his birthday? My mind started racing!

What do I do about a gift? Should I run out to the car to see if I have something that hasn't been opened or used? Maybe a book? Talking to myself out loud at this point, "What are you thinking, Jeremy? He doesn't need a book from you; he's written three!" (Side note: you're only considered crazy when you start answering yourself) I paused… Then I remembered a story from Estes. He told me about his mentor, Paul Orberson. That led me to wonder if Clifton was also a fan of peanut butter and Diet Sunkist. But how many people do you know who carry those two items around in their car in case of an emergency *It's My Mentor's Birthday & I Just Found Out* situation? Yeah, exactly… Nobody!

I gathered myself, and when the server dropped by, I asked her to bring out a slice of cherry pie. I thought that would suffice. You may be thinking that was a corny move, but that's all I could do with what I had where I was at. I honestly don't think Art Williams yelling out, "All you can do is all you can do!," is the first thing that would cross someone's mind in this situation, but it did. I'll admit - I'm a personal development junkie. And when that slice of pie popped off the page, I thought, *if this guy doesn't like cherry pie he's crazy!* (Nevermind the fact that I was the one who was still talking to myself) Then, I asked for a slice of pecan pie, just in case he wanted to trade. It's never a bad idea to have a Plan B.

Do you see where I'm going here? I was tore up from the floor up - literally tripping out. One other thing was certain, though; I was excited! As he walked in, towering above everyone, I noticed quickly that he was excited too. I stood to greet him. Then it dawned on me as we shook hands, while he was grinning from ear to ear, handing me a gift bag full of books, that successful people love giving back to others. That message was written all over him.

He taught me in one brief moment, that winners love to be asked, "How did you do it? What was your reason why?" They want to share their story. They want to help the young person who aspires to do more, be more and achieve more. **But most people never ASK.** And if you ask not, you have not.

Clifton Lambreth had the perspective I needed. He even had time to consider my questions (I emailed them days in advance). It was such a profound meeting for me because he had exactly what I wanted. It didn't take me long to figure that out when I was introduced to him in the summer of 2013 while helping some business partners with a small training at the lovely home of Dr. Ron and Julie Derr (two of my favorite people on the planet). He mentioned working early in his career for Zig Ziglar and everything he said that day to me was worth its weight in gold. That's the day I collected his contact information.

As he took his seat, he said, "This is one of my favorite spots, so I'm ready to order when you are, Chief." Clifton's nonchalantness (if that's even a word) brought a calm over me. I realized that we were much more alike than we were different. We worked through some questions over our meal. He would occasionally insist, "Write this down." But what I was most drawn to was that everything - I mean everything - turned into a story. When I checked my phone, several sweet teas later, it was almost 3:00!

Here was a gentleman who had just returned home from North Carolina on a speaking engagement and he showed up to meet me on his birthday. Most people would've politely declined my request.

He brought me a stack of books, suggested readings, that included works from the likes of Russell H. Cromwell and Ken Blanchard. "Here, read these," he said. "This will help you get the ball rolling."

I stepped out of the restaurant that day a different person than when I walked in. As I pulled up directions for my departure on the trusty smartphone, he walked by my shiny, brand new Mountain Grey Metallic CLA 250 Mercedes-Benz. He tapped my front passenger side window, and raising his voice so I didn't have to lower the window, he asked, "Is that your *$FREE.99-Benz*?" I signaled yes with a smile and a head nod, and he hit me back with a thumbs up. I leaned back in my seat to get a glimpse of what luxury car he was cruising in, and to my surprise, I saw him unlock the door of what was an older model Ford Taurus. That then changed the name of the slice of pecan pie I had earlier to "humble pie" instead. And as a side note: the birthday cherry pie worked out well!

Opening my notebook before pulling out of the parking lot, I revisited the pearls he shared:

> *... One word at a time. Whatever God places on your heart, share that... If you're all in, God's going to tell you to go*

places when everyone else is telling you not to. Rarely will you have what you need in order to do what you feel you have to do, but if you trust God, He will provide... He'll bring you along. He goes before you and He is with you. Just make sure you do your part. It won't be easy, but you do have what it takes. Your test will become your testimony and your mess will become your message... Focus on serving others. Give away what you have - your time, your talent, your treasure, and your touch... And every single day: get up, dress up, show up and don't give up.

I'd say it was a productive lunch. What about you?

For people who are running toward their dreams, life has a special kind of meaning.
-Les Brown

Resources

Barca, J. (2010, December 1). J.J. Watt: Delivering Pizza to Reach the NFL. Retrieved from http://jerrybarca.com/writing/j-j-watt-delivering-pizza-to-reach-the-nfl

Batterson, M. (2006). *In a Pit with a Lion on a Snowy Day: How to Survive and Thrive When Opportunity Roars* (p. 144). Colorado Springs: Multnomah Books.

Batterson, M. (2011). *Soul Print: Discovering Your Divine Destiny* (p. 19). Colorado Springs: Multnomah Books.

Dungy, T. (2011). *The One Year Uncommon Life Daily Challenge* (p. March 30). Winter Park: Tyndale.

Golden, M. (2007). *From the Trash Man to the Cash Man: How Anyone Can Get Rich Starting from Anywhere* (p. 25). New Kingston: Skillionaire Enterprises.

Olson, J. (2005). *The Slight Edge: Turning Simple Decisions Into Massive Success* (Revised Edition ed., p. 124). Lake Dallas: SUCCESS Books.

Lechter, S., & Reid, G. (2009). Foreword by Mark Victor Hansen. In *Three Feet from Gold: Turn Your Obstacles into Opportunities!* (p. Xii). New York: Sterling.

Mackintosh, A. (2014, January 1). Our Story. Retrieved from http://www.aberdeengreenmusic.com

Maxwell, J. (2000). *Failing Forward: Turning Mistakes into Stepping Stones for Success* (p. 42, 116). Nashville: Thomas Nelson.

Maxwell, J. (2012). *The 15 Invaluable Laws of Growth: Live Them and Reach Your Potential* (p. 203, 225). Nashville: Center Street.

Newton, J. (n.d.). Amazing Grace Lyrics. Retrieved from http://www.constitution.org/col/amazing_grace.htm

Roenigk, A. (2014, November 4). Hill fulfills dream, nets 4 points. Retrieved from http://www.espn.go.com/ncw/story?story=11809823&src=desktop

Wilkinson, B. (2000). *The Prayer of Jabez: Breaking Through to the Blessed Life* (p. 41). Colorado Springs: Multnomah Books.

Jones, C. (1968). *Life is Tremendous* (p. 25). Mechanicsburg: Executive Books.

Harman, Steve. CBS News. <https://www.cbsnews.com/news/former-nfl-player-farms-for-good> November 14, 2014.

About the Author

Jeremy Taylor is a highly sought after keynote and inspirational speaker. He was born and raised in Campbellsville, Kentucky, where he graduated from Taylor County High School and Campbellsville University. Soon after the start of his teaching and coaching career, he decided to pursue his passion of encouraging people by following his entrepreneurial spirit. He's now built a thriving global network marketing business in the health and wellness industry and is the founder and CEO of Jeremy And You. Jeremy resides in Bowling Green, Kentucky, where he enjoys serving his community as an active member of Living Hope Baptist Church. Jesus, people, food, traveling, reading and sports are all some of Jeremy's favorites. He believes in keeping the main thing *the main thing* and, **"if you're not having fun, you're not doing it right!"**

Connect with Jeremy and follow him at…

Twitter & Instagram: @jermataylor
Facebook: jeremy.taylor.12177
Website: jeremyandyou.com

Please share this book with someone you love!

Made in the USA
Charleston, SC
23 January 2015